REFLECTIONS FOR THE SOUL

Victor S E Moubarak

Copyright © 2015 by Victor S E Moubarak

REFLECTIONS FOR THE SOUL
By Victor S E Moubarak

All rights reserved solely by the author. The author guarantees all contents are original and do not infringe upon the legal rights of any other person or work. No part of this book may be reproduced in any form without the permission of the author. The views expressed in this book are not necessarily those of the publisher.

A selection of readings to help you reflect and meditate when praying or when in need of inspiration. You can read the reflections in chronological order or just open the book at any page and read what is there. Hopefully, it will help you in your prayers. The author uses humour where appropriate to deliver a memorable message. You may find a hidden gem in what he writes.

Also by Victor S E Moubarak

"VISIONS"
ISBN 978 1 60477 032 2

"VISIONS" is a fictional story of three children who see an apparition of the Lord Jesus on their way to church. They tell their priest, Father Ignatius, about it; and pretty soon news spreads throughout town.

People react to the news in different ways. Some readily believe; others mock and scoff in disbelief, whilst some react violently towards the children and their families.

Parishioners seek guidance from Father Ignatius whereas the Church seeks to hush the whole story in the hope that it goes away; whilst Jesus appears again and again.

"VISIONS" challenges readers to ask what they would do in a similar situation – as Christians, as parents or just as onlookers.

A vibrant tale of supernatural events, with a fast-paced storyline and strong believable characters, "VISIONS" is a challenging must-read Christian book for everyone ready for a reality check on what they actually believe.

"VISIONS" is available in paperback from AMAZON and all good bookstores and on the Internet. It is also available in Kindle, Nook and other electronic versions.

"THE PRIEST AND PROSTITUTE"
ISBN-10: 150106570X
ISBN-13: 978-1501065705

When Father Ignatius is suspected of murder his whole life is turned upside down. His Faith takes a real shaking as he tries in vain to plead his innocence. The Church is shaken to its very foundations and his parishioners jump to as many conclusions as they can find and start judging without any facts or evidence.

This is the time for the priest to find out who his real friends are. Or are they keeping close to him for ulterior motives?

"THE PRIEST AND PROSTITUTE" is a fast-paced story with believable characters and situations. A realistic self-test as to one's faith and beliefs, as well as the ability to stay focused on God when it seems He has abandoned you.

"GOD'S SHEPHERD"
ISBN-10: 1500683957
ISBN-13: 978-1500683955

Father Ignatius, the Parish priest at St Vincent Church is an amiable soul whose kind and jovial personality is well loved and appreciated by his parishioners and all those who know him. His is not a nine-to-five job where he can get home on time for his evening meal and a good evening watching TV, or playing golf. He is always "on-call" so to speak having to attend to his flock when in trouble and difficulties, or having to go to hospital at all hours of day and night when someone is gravely ill.

"GOD'S SHEPHERD" is a collection of short stories specially selected by the author as amongst his favourites. They tell of the day to day adventures of a gentle pious priest with a gift of dispensing good advice and wise lessons to a troubled world.

"TO LOVE A PRIEST"
ISBN: 978 1 505 908558

When Father Ignatius' past catches up with him there is no way to escape the consequences for him and those around him. He must face facts regardless of how seriously they could affect his vocation as a priest.

"TO LOVE A PRIEST" is the most controversial book in the Father Ignatius series and deals with questions on many peoples' minds as yet unresolved by the Church. A gripping story of conflict between conscience and dogma, treating a delicate subject with compassion and forgiveness.

****

I hope that you enjoy all books which I've authored and that perhaps they may bring someone somewhere to get to experience God's love.

I pray that God blesses each one of you dear readers, old and new, and may He be with you and your families always.

Victor S E Moubarak

www.holyvisions.co.uk and www.holyvisions.uk

WHO DO YOU THINK I AM?

In Matthew Chapter 16 verse 13 onwards we read that Jesus asked His disciples "Who do you say I am?"

Peter answered quite rightly, "You are the Messiah, the Son of the living God".

I now ask you "Who do you think you are?"

I am not asking you for your name, the name of your parents, or your family lineage. I am not asking you whether you are male or female, single, married, divorced, separated or in partnership with anyone. Whether you are a parent or uncle, aunt or whatever. I am not even asking you whether you are a doctor, nurse, lawyer, carpenter or whatever your job may be; if you have one.

I am asking you "Who do you think you are?"

Do you really know yourself? To know oneself deeply and fully we should consider "what makes us tick". What is it that makes us who we are, or what we have become as we grew up, or as we are still growing up.

We are all the product of our background, environment, parentage, up-bringing and a variety of other factors that make us what we are now. But have we ever taken the time to consider how these factors have affected us and made us what we are today?

Take for instance our opinions on any subject. Our views. Our prejudices (for we all have them no matter what we lead others to believe). Our fears real or imagined. Are these all of our own making or are they pre-set opinions or views we have heard or learnt from others and adapted them to suit our own beliefs and requirements?

How many of our views and opinions are indeed logically assessed and formulated by us as opposed to following someone else's views?

Let's go back to the Scripture quoted above. If Jesus challenged us and asked "Who do you say I am?" What would our honest, no hesitation, response be?

Can we say in all honesty that He is the Son of God? Or is there some hesitation in our voice?

And if He asked "Who do you think you are?" What would our answer be?

Whatever our opinion of ourselves may be, or whatever or whoever we think we are. One think is for sure. We are all the Creations of God. Indeed we are the sons and daughters of God.

Why else would we call Him Father when we recite the Lord's Prayer?

And no matter what faults we may think we have, physical or otherwise; we are all loved by God our Creator and we are perfect in His eyes.

Because there are no rejects on God's production line!

THIS MAN

Let's role play for a moment or so.

Imagine you're a person of authority in a Court of Law. The judge, the final arbiter, whatever you say happens.

And they bring to you a man. He is fairly ordinary looking and they accuse Him of saying He is the Son of God. And this is blasphemy according to the Law and He should be put to death.

Before you make such a momentous decision on the man's life, you decide to do some investigations.

You check and you find that this man has been around for about three years or so. He has been travelling up and down the land, and He has indeed said several times that He is the Son of God. He preaches to people and He tells them to repent from their sins and to follow the Way of the Lord.

So you wonder about this and you think "Well, maybe if I can prove that this man is mad, I could let Him off. I could tell the people that He is insane, and they should let Him go, and I could warn Him not to repeat what He says because it would get Him into deep trouble".

So you check on the man's sanity and you find that indeed He is not mad at all. Many people can testify to the fact that He has preached in the temples, and He has debated with religious elders, and shows no sign of being mentally insane whatsoever. Indeed, He is very wise.

And you also find that this man seems to have some supernatural powers because He has healed many people up and down the country. The blind can see, the deaf can hear, the dumb can talk and the lame can walk. And there's plenty of evidence for what He has done. There's even a Roman Officer who can testify that He has healed. What better evidence do you want?

And also, you understand that apparently He has raised people from the dead. Now that's very strange. No one has ever done that before. But again there's plenty of evidence of that. There's the family of a man called Lazarus who apparently had died and had been entombed for a few days yet Jesus raised him from the dead and raised other people from the dead.

And when He preaches He says to people "Your Faith has saved you" whatever that means. And He heals them. He doesn't charge at all for what He is doing. He just wants people to repent and follow the Lord.

So you wonder whether He's some sort of trickster, some sort of charlatan. So you order your soldiers to beat Him up and to rough Him a bit to see whether He admits to being a liar, a cheat.

Your soldiers torture Him, beat Him up, they put a crown of thorns on His head because He claims to being a King of some sort. But after all that the man still does not say anything in His defence.

So you give up. You think, "Well, He is one of their people. He is not one of us. So what's it to do with me if they want to kill Him."

So you give orders for Him to be put to death.

Your soldiers put a Cross on His back and get Him to carry it all the way to the place where He is nailed to that Cross and left there to die.

And just before He dies He asks God in Heaven to forgive these people, because they don't know what they are doing.

What's more strange is that three days later this very man is Himself raised from the dead. And a lot of people see Him and can testify to His Resurrection.

Now I wonder. Is this enough evidence that this man is really the Son of God?

Because it is for me.

THE LAZARUS EPISODE

The story of the death of Lazarus and his bringing back to life by Jesus is strange indeed. It is not like any other story of Christ's miracles. There are at least two important lessons for us to learn here.

Let's recap quickly (John Chapter 11).

Jesus was in a town not far from Bethany when He receives a message from Martha and Mary that their brother Lazarus is ill. Jesus does not hurry to heal Lazarus but He stays put. He tells His disciples that this illness will not result in Lazarus' death. The disciples, as ever, do not understand. They think that Lazarus has fallen asleep because of his illness. Jesus spells it out "Lazarus is dead!" and then decides to go to him.

When He arrives at Bethany, followed by His disciples, Jesus is met by Martha.

She is full of grief at her brother's death. She sent a message to Jesus two days earlier and now He comes. When it's too late. She says to Jesus "If you had been here, Lord, my brother would not have died!"

She reprimands Jesus. In her grief, she does not know what to say.

Then she adds, "But I know that even now God will give you whatever you ask Him for". She still believes that God can do anything through Jesus.

LESSON 1

When we are in great grief, or despair, we sometimes lash out at God. We blame Him for what has happened. This is only natural. It is our human nature speaking.

God knows that and He can take our anger. After all, He took all our anger and hatred when He hung there from the Cross.

Like in Martha's case, God forgives. We should in return hold on to our Faith and believe that everything is possible to God.

Mary joins her sister to meet Jesus and she too says "If you had been here Lazarus would not have died". The crowd murmurs that Jesus healed many sick people, why did He not come earlier to save Lazarus.

Jesus asks for the tomb to be opened. Martha tells Him that there will be a bad smell. Lazarus has been buried for four days. In a hot climate the body would have began to smell badly. The tomb is opened and Jesus raises Lazarus.

LESSON 2

Why did Jesus take so long to visit Lazarus? Why wait four days after his death and burial to turn up?

In the past, Jesus raised many people from the dead. So why did He wait so long this time?

In previous miracles, many skeptics and cynics would have said that the individual was probably not dead. He may have been in a deep sleep, or in a coma. Not much of a miracle.

This time Jesus waited for four days after death and burial to turn up and raise Lazarus. He wanted there to be no doubt that Lazarus is dead and that he has been raised back to life. No doubt that God's glory, through Him, will be seen by everyone.

He predicted from the very start, when He heard that Lazarus was ill, that he would not end up dead. The disciples did not understand, but Jesus explained that Lazarus was indeed dead; but will not end up dead.

His words "The final result of this illness will not be the death of Lazarus; this has happened in order to bring glory to God, and it will be the means by which the Son of God will receive glory."

Our lesson is to learn that when things go wrong ... very ... very wrong; we need only believe that the end result will be that God is glorified, as is His will.

WHY THINGS GO WRONG

God does not make bad things happen to us. He does not play games with us and watches how we react to situations. He allows bad things to happen, for reasons best known to Himself, which (for now) we are not meant to understand. He allows bad things to happen because it is His will.

More often than not, when bad things happen it is because of our actions, or in-actions. We start the ball rolling by the actions we take as humans. Again, God allows that to happen. He gave us free will and in His generosity and kindness He allows us a free hand to do what we want; even though sometimes what we want and do results in bad things happening.

The question then is: WHY does He allow bad things to happen? If He loves us so much why does He not protect us from all evil?

Of course, most of the time He DOES protect us from evil. It is, after all, part of our Lord's Prayer when we petition Him. He protects us from more evils than we could imagine, often without us even knowing that we need such protection.

Yet ... He allows bad things to happen. Why? Perhaps to give us all an opportunity to love one another and to help one another. When something bad happens, say a disaster for instance, famine, floods and so on; this is our opportunity to do something to help our fellow man. How else would we obey His Commandment of loving one another if we had no opportunity to do so?

Perhaps we are not meant to know why God allows bad things to happen. But this should not stop us from loving and helping one another.

WHEN THINGS GO WRONG

God allows bad things to happen. He does not make them happen.

More often than not, when bad things happen, our knee-jerk reaction is to blame God.

God allows these things to happen to serve His own purpose in His own time and in His own way. We really do not know why He allows them to happen; but we must trust Him.

When bad things happen, it is important to remember that God is still in control. He knows what has happened, how it affects people close to the event, and even people far away and totally detached from it. He never loses control of the situation.

Our reaction to these events is therefore vital. Our human nature will take over and all our emotions will come to the fore – shock, fear, denial, anger and so on.

However, when we have calmed down a little, we should turn to God and praise and thank Him.

"What did you just say? Praise Him?"

We are praising and thanking Him for still being in control of the situation - not because He allowed the bad thing to happen.

Our praise acknowledges His supreme power over the whole universe. We are in effect saying that we accept that He allowed the bad things to happen, yet we still trust Him, and trust that His will be done.

When we acknowledge, in such terrible situations, that His will is still paramount; we open a channel, in certain circumstances, for Him to turn the situation to the good.

I have seen this happen several times.

CAN WE REALLY TRUST GOD?

It is natural, of course, for children to trust their parents. They accept without questioning that their parents love them and will "not give them a stone if they ask for bread" or "give them a snake when they ask for a fish" (Luke 11:11).

This natural trust which we all have at birth continues as we grow up until some day someone hurts us for the first time. We become wary and careful to protect our vulnerability. Our trust dies a little. We become more selective in whom we trust and how much we trust different people.

It is in our nature to be careful and self-protective in this way. To trust everyone explicitly without question borders on immaturity or naivety to the extreme.

So, how do we get to totally trust an unseen God? A God we have grown to believe in; and we claim that He loves us and has our best interest at heart?

How do we trust Him when/if we've experienced frequent un-answered prayers; or when things go wrong in our lives?

Sure, it is easy to say glibly "Trust in God", "He wants the best for us", "He loves us", and so on, when things are going well in our lives.

But at what point do we really trust Him above all else and say "Thy will be done" and honestly mean it?

Regardless of the outcome of the situation, however bad it may be, are we really able to trust Him all the same? Because we know deep in our hearts that He will see us through our current difficulties.

It seems impossible doesn't it? To totally trust an unseen God without question. Just like a child.

But we have examples of others who have done just that.

The Virgin Mary trusted Him so much that she declared "let it be as God says", when she was visited by the Angel Gabriel.

Joseph trusted Him too when he took Mary as his wife.

Paul, Peter and the other early followers of Christ trusted Him too even when thrown into jail several times, were beaten, persecuted, stoned and put to death. They didn't say "Enough with all that. God has let us down many times and allowed us to be imprisoned and beaten."

They still held on to their trust. Even to the point of death itself. They still trusted God and His Son Jesus.

How?

I suppose it is by surrendering their all to God. Literally giving their everything, their lives even, to God, in the full knowledge that, whatever happens, it will be for the good. They literally accepted that their lives were not their own and that their God, the God in Whom they trusted, would protect them even if it meant that they would die for Him.

These days of macho-liberated culture, we tend to consider surrender as a weakness.

In fact it is a strength.

Can you imagine the will-power and concentration of mind required to say "I totally trust you God, no matter what happens. You will look after me and my loved ones"?

And really believe it ... yes, really and truly believe it.

To be one thousand per cent certain that all will turn out all right?

This is no sign of weakness, no sign of surrender; but an act of strength and faith in the extreme.

To many this may seem impossible. Too difficult a proposition. Against our very nature to be wary and suspicious.

Perhaps so. But it should not stop us from trying.

And when our trust falters. When we hesitate and perhaps our "inner voice" makes us doubt His true love. We stop, ask His forgiveness, and start once again.

Through His grace He will lift us up and renew our trust in Him once again.

BASIC INSTINCTS

We all act on instinct from time to time. If we touch something hot or sharp we immediately withdraw in pain. If we taste something unpleasant, the basic instinct is to spit it out. And when I hammer hard on my finger, missing the nail altogether, as I did this morning, believe me, my first instinct was not to say: "Jolly gosh, this was a tad uncomfortable for me !!!".

I suppose the same applies when some terrible situation happens to us. The first instinct is probably fear, followed with a multitude of others such as confusion, doubts, worry, anger and so on.

But what if our first instinct in such situations was to immediately turn to God?

Instinctively, without thinking, turn to God for help, reassurance, guidance and peace.

What if our automatic reflex to any bad situation was an immediate reaching out to God? Before even the negative emotions come into play.

Wouldn't that make our lives that much better? Because after all, God's will for us is to have peace. Christ often greeted His disciples with the words "Peace be with you".

So at the first sign of trouble, let's turn to Him and ask: "Lord, grant me your peace in this situation."

Years ago I knew a priest who was always calm and serene. Nothing seemed to rattle him, and I truly believe he had the Holy Spirit within him.

Once in a sermon he said: "I've made a deal with God. I carry out His work on earth to the best of my abilities; He takes care of the worries!"

There's a message for us to consider here.

GIVING UP

It happens to all of us I suppose at one time or another.

We try to achieve something, but the more we try the more we fail.
We try again and again and we fail one more time. We're so tired of
trying to achieve our goal that we feel like giving up.

It is said that on His way to Calvary Jesus fell to the ground three
times. It is not Biblical of course, but we can assume that He must
have stumbled or fallen at least once.

He was exhausted. He had been beaten, mocked, spat upon and
tortured. His disciples had run away in fear, one of whom even
denied Him three times. He must have been totally exhausted
carrying His Cross up that hill.

That's enough to make anybody give up.

Jesus could have stayed there on the ground and died on the spot.
But He got up. Three times. He got up and continued His journey to
a cruel and very painful death.

He did it for us. He did it because His Father asked Him to.

Let that be our inspiration to try once again when we feel like giving
up.

DON'T PANIC ... DON'T PANIC

Crises will happen to us from time to time. God permits them for His own purpose and for His own reasons.

Our natural reaction may be to panic.

Our un-natural reaction is to remain calm. Take a deep breath and trust in God.

At times of crisis we need to proceed slowly, in the conscious knowledge that God is with us and will protect us.

I repeat: in the conscious knowledge.

We should speak our truth quietly, as the opportunity arises, and as the Holy Spirit guides us.

We should avoid needless talk, or needless worries and concerns. But nurture a peace in our hearts that comes from Him, who cares and will protect us. If we allow Him to.

Our prayers should be focused on His will, and His plans for us in this critical situation; in the sure belief that He will see us through it just as He has brought us to it.

IF YOU DON'T BELIEVE … LEAVE

John Chapter 6 has been the source of much debate and confusion over the years ... and the arguments will still go on. No doubt to the amusement of Jesus looking down upon us and saying: "You of little Faith. Why can't you just believe and stop dissecting and analyzing everything I said as if I were an insect in your lab!"

I speak of course of the part in that Chapter where Jesus says He is "the Bread of life" and later when He says that unless people eat His flesh or drink His blood they will not have life.

As you can imagine, this was very confusing to His listeners; even His followers and disciples.

"What is He on about?" they asked. "How can we eat His flesh and drink His blood? This is cannibalism surely. This is too much for us. We don't want to follow this guy any longer!"

So what did Jesus do?

He didn't say "Hey ... wait a minute. You didn't understand what I meant. This is what I really meant to say ... let me explain!"

No ... Jesus let them go. He didn't try to justify Himself or what He had just said. It was as if He dissolved the unspoken contract between them. They could not accept a certain clause so He let them go.

Then He turned to His disciples and asked: "How about you? Do you want to go as well?"

As ever, Peter was first to answer: "To whom shall we go?" he asked. "We're in this for the duration, all the way, to the end". Or words to that effect, signifying that he trusted Jesus without question; albeit no doubt he had many questions in his mind. Peter accepted Christ's words without question and stepped out in blind Faith and dared to believe.

So what are we to make of all this after all these years? Did Jesus mean what He said literally or was it all symbolism and imagery using common day articles of the time like bread and wine to signify the sacrifice He is to endure for us? His flesh would be torn by the beating and the nailing to the Cross and His blood would be spilled for us. Was it all symbolism?

Quite frankly, I'm with Peter on this.

I don't believe there is much to be gained in debating this ad-infinitum because in reality I doubt any of us will ever come to a satisfactory conclusion. Wiser heads than mine have argued this matter over the centuries much to the amusement of Jesus looking down from above. Any efforts by me at interpreting this would no doubt have Jesus rolling on the floor with laughter.

So I am minded to accept it for what it is. Something that Jesus said and we're to believe it as best we humanly can.

There's no point in closing your eyes tightly and repeating over and over again "I believe ... I believe ... even though I don't understand it ... I believe".

God who can see deep within our hearts, and knows our human nature and its failings, realizes that it is too difficult for us to understand.

But then, He does not ask us to understand Him. He asks us to love Him and to trust Him without any evidence whatsoever.

It's what is called Faith.

To believe when your common sense tells you not to.

CREDO

Every large Organization or institution has a Mission Statement. A statement outlining what the Organization is set up to do, what are its values, ethics, and purpose.

Many years ago, in the year 325, the first Ecumenical Council of Churches met and wrote a "mission statement" which is better known as the Nicene Creed. The name originates from the city of Nicaea in Turkey, where the Ecumenical Council met.

Also known as the Credo, (I believe), this document or statement has been accepted by most Christian denominations in the world.

It is, in fact, what a Christian truly believes. It is what identifies a Christian from anyone else.

Let's look at it in some detail:

I believe in one God, the Father Almighty.

This proclaims at the onset that there is only one God. We are taught to see Him and address Him as a Father. A symbol of love, caring, mercy and forgiveness. And that He is almighty; not like any other father here on earth.

Maker of Heaven and earth, and of all things visible and invisible.

He is so almighty that He has made everything. Visible and invisible. This bit is important. It says visible and invisible. Not seen and unseen. If I were to leave one room and enter another I become unseen. But I am not invisible.

The use of the word invisible is to underline the fact that there is an invisible, spiritual, world which we do not see. We are both visible in human form and invisible in our spiritual form - our soul.

There is also an invisible world of angels and spirits of those departed from this world. As well, of course, as the invisible Holy Spirit.

And in one Lord Jesus Christ, the only begotten Son of God, and born of the Father before all ages. God of God, light of light, true God of true God. Begotten not made, consubstantial to the Father, by whom all things were made.

Note in particular that we say one Lord Jesus Christ. He is our Lord, our Master, and there is no other.

Begotten - born of a Father (God) - not made by God just as He made us, and the planets and everything else.

Before all ages. Jesus has always existed. He did not just begin to exist when He was born on earth. This is when He appeared to us in human form. But before that, He has always existed with God, because He is God.

Consubstantial to the Father. From Latin consubstantialem, of one essence or substance. This word was used by the Council of Nicaea (325) to express the Divinity of Christ. The Trinity is not a hierarchy. It isn't God at the top, then Jesus, and then the Holy Spirit. All three are equal and one; and have always been so.

Who for us men and for our salvation came down from Heaven. And was incarnate of the Holy Ghost and of the Virgin Mary and was made man;

Another proclamation that Jesus, who always existed, became human form through the Holy Spirit and the Virgin Mary.

was crucified also for us under Pontius Pilate, suffered and was buried; and the third day rose again according to the Scriptures.

What is Pilate doing here? Why is he getting a mention in the Creed?

This is very important and significant. Jesus' life, death and resurrection is not some fairy story we hear and tell our children. "Once upon a time ..."

This is actual fact and it happened at a point in time. When Pilate was ruler. The mention of Pilate is to serve as a beacon in history so that future readers reciting the Creed can identify when these real facts actually happened.

Jesus died and rose again as predicted in the Old Testament by the prophets.

And ascended into Heaven, sits at the right hand of the Father, and shall come again with glory to judge the living and the dead, of whose Kingdom there shall be no end.

Jesus is indeed King in Heaven with God. We also believe that He is with us here and now in Spiritual form. Always by our side and ready to help us with our needs.

But we also believe that He will return to earth in human form as He did all those years ago.

And I believe in the Holy Ghost, the Lord and Giver of life, who proceeds from the Father and the Son, who together with the Father and the Son is to be adored and glorified, who spoke by the prophets.

Another proclamation that the Holy Spirit is one with the Father and the Son.

The Holy Spirit has always existed. Just like God and Jesus.

He inspired the prophets to write what they wrote, and to predict the birth, life, death and resurrection of Jesus. The prophets did not make it all up as a fairy story. They were told by the Holy Spirit what to write.

And the holy, catholic and apostolic Church.

The word holy does not refer to us. There are plenty of so-called Christians who are far from holy! This refers to the Church. It was created by Jesus through Peter and it is holy because of this.

Catholic means throughout the world, universal. (Katholikos from katholou).

Apostolic means belonging and starting from the Apostles as chosen by Christ.

I confess one baptism for the remission of sins.

If we are to be put right with God we just have to accept Him through baptism and to confess and be sorry for our sins.

And I look for the resurrection of the dead and the life of the world to come.

This is yet again very significant. Here we proclaim that this life, in this world, is only a passing phase. When we die there will be a resurrection and a new spiritual life in a spiritual world.

THE HOLY TRINITY

For centuries people have been trying to comprehend the mystery of the Holy Trinity as if it is a puzzle which we are meant to resolve, and when we do we get a prize.

God the Father, Jesus the Son, and the Holy Spirit ... (no title) ... three in one. What is that supposed to mean?

We accept, (those of us who believe), that God exists and is up there somewhere, in Heaven, above the clouds or wherever. He has always existed and has created us, as well as everything else in the Universe and beyond. OK ... we can understand and believe that.

Then there is Jesus. Born as a baby of a Virgin by the power of the Holy Spirit, and came to earth as a human. OK ... so He is the Son of God.

But wait a minute ... in the Credo it says I believe "in one Lord Jesus Christ, the only begotten Son of God, and born of the Father before all ages. God of God, light of light, true God of true God. Begotten not made, consubstantial to the Father, by whom all things were made."

Jesus was begotten, not made by God just like He made us and everything else. "Before all ages" - this means that Jesus has always existed. He did not just begin to exist when He was born on earth. When He was born on earth is when He appeared to us in human form. But before that, He has always existed with God, because He is God.

Consubstantial to the Father. From Latin consubstantialem, of one essence or substance. This word was used by the Council of Nicaea (325) when they wrote the Credo to express the Divinity of Christ. The Trinity is not a hierarchy. It isn't God at the top, then Jesus, and then the Holy Spirit. All three are equal and one; and have always been so.

Confusing? I suppose it is. But there's more.

We are then told about the Holy Spirit. He is the Spirit of God - His soul perhaps. He doesn't have a title as such. God is God, the Creator, our Father in Heaven. Jesus is His only Son, our Saviour. But the Holy Spirit ... no title!

It was St Hilary of Poitiers, a Bishop in the 3rd Century AD, who first described the Holy Spirit as 'the gift'. He is the gift given to us by God after Jesus ascended into Heaven. He is the very Spirit of God Himself. His very soul, come back to us on earth to dwell within us and to help us in our Christian life. That's why He is sometimes referred to as the Helper, the Counsellor, God's own Being living within us.

And that is the Holy Trinity which we believe in and perhaps don't understand.

But let's be honest, there are many men in this world who, after years of marriage, still do not understand their wives; so what hope have we really got of understanding the Holy Trinity?

When we get to meet St Peter we will not sit an exam to check how much we have learnt and what we understand.

God will instead look into our hearts ... our Faith ... and our actions.

God does not ask us to understand Him ... He asks us to trust Him and love Him.

THE HOLY TRINITY – HISTORICAL EXPLANATION

One of the great mysteries of our Faith is the Holy Trinity. No matter how much we may scratch our heads, I doubt we'll be able to understand it. Not that we are meant to, I suppose.

Let's see if this can explain it a little.

For years on end in the Old Testament times people believed in one God. Leaders like Abraham, Moses and David believed in one living God; only one Person.

In those days, there were people who believed in many gods of course. So if God had revealed Himself to the Jews as three Persons in one, and assuming they understood this, (we don't understand it ourselves now), then the pagans would have thought that the Jews believed in three gods.

Later on, at the times of the New Testament, the apostles, who were Jews, believed from childhood that there was only one Person in God. That's what they had learnt from the writings of the Old Testament prophets and that's what they experienced in their lives. They saw God's hand in everything that happened. He was the God of Abraham, Moses and David. The God written about in history. The God up there in Heaven who gave them the moral law, (Commandments), and who created everything.

Then one day they met a Man named Jesus. For three years they lived with Him.

They saw that He spoke with authority and conviction, and all that He said made sense. They watched how He lived and the way He related to people.

He showed compassion for the sick, the destitute and those forgotten by society. He cared for the hungry and the poor and showed kindness for everybody.

When anyone was rude or insulting to Him, He did not answer back in anger.

He lived His life on a high moral plain but showed sympathy and understanding for those who were stained and scarred by sin.

He taught them about His Father who was God and that He was the Son of God. One day, when He asked them who they thought He was, Peter was quick to answer "You are the Christ, the Son of the living God."

They saw Him perform many miracles. They saw Him die and then alive again, and knew He had conquered death and the grave. Time and again they saw Him after the Resurrection, spoke with Him and ate with Him.

It was impossible for them to think or talk about God without thinking and talking about Jesus. They had come to know God their Father through His Son.

When Jesus was taken up to Heaven after the Resurrection the disciples were distraught. What are they to do now? Their Leader whom they saw and trusted all these years had gone. They were afraid, so they hid in houses secretly, wondering what to do next.

As promised, Jesus sent His Holy Spirit, the Comforter, upon them nine days later.

Their eyes were opened and they believed, and understood, that He was the Third Person of God.

Today, many people don't understand the Holy Spirit, but you can rest assured that those early Christians understood Him all right.

Because they had experienced Him. He became such a force in their lives, giving them strength to spread the Good News that Jesus had taught them, enabling them to live as Jesus had lived.

It was they who handed on to us this mystery that in one God there are three Persons.

ADVOCATE? WHAT ADVOCATE?

'If you love me, you will keep my commandments. And I will ask the Father, and He will give you another Advocate, to be with you for ever. This is the Spirit of truth, whom the world cannot receive, because it neither sees Him nor knows Him. You know Him, because He abides with you, and He will be in you.' John 14:15-17

Who is this Advocate? Some might ask.

Jesus here is speaking of the Holy Spirit. The Spirit of God, and Jesus Himself, who will come down from Heaven at Pentecost and be within the disciples.

There's often confusion in people's minds about the Holy Spirit. Who is He exactly?

We are taught about God the Father, Jesus the Son, and the Holy Spirit … He doesn't seem to have a title or description.

St Hilary of Poitiers, a Bishop in the 3rd Century AD, described the Holy Spirit as "the Gift".

He is the Gift given to us by God after Jesus ascended into Heaven.

He is the very Spirit of God, God Himself, come back to us on earth to dwell within us and to help us in our Christian life.

That's why He is sometimes referred to as the Helper, the Counselor, God's own Being living within us.

The Holy Spirit didn't just descend on the disciples at Pentecost and that's it. A once in a lifetime event. He is present here and now, today, and is within some people who ask for His presence within them.

Now that last fact itself, God's own Being living within us, causes even more confusion amongst Christians and non-Christians alike.

Sure, Christians believe the Holy Spirit descended upon the disciples at Pentecost teaching them what to say in various languages and how to proclaim the Good News to all. But now? Today? Does the Holy Spirit enter our very souls today?

Can you imagine that?

God. Living within us. Guiding us. Helping us. Teaching us. Advising us when to speak and when to remain silent. What to say and what to do.

Isn't that wonderful? Or is it too difficult to imagine or believe?

If you were to say to a non-Christian that God is living within you in the form of the Holy Spirit they would most probably scoff, or smile politely, or perhaps think you've lost your mind. The very concept is difficult for many Christians to believe; never mind those who don't believe at all.

Isn't it a tragedy that in this day and age, people can and do believe that the devil can possess an individual unwillingly and reap havoc in their lives; but yet they find it difficult to understand that the Spirit of God is willing to abide within us and lead us to an eternal better life in Heaven.

But only if we ask Him.

Unlike the devil, the Holy Spirit will not abide in a person unless He is asked. Unless He is invited.

All we have to do is to believe and to invite the Holy Spirit to be within us.

GOD RELATIONSHIP

Intelligence and knowledge increases from one generation to the next. What you and I know, our parents didn't. And what our parents knew, their parents and grandparents didn't.

The same applies to relationships and the nature of relationships, I suppose.

Some people today have a personal relationship with God and His Son Jesus. They are not just characters in a book, or in the Bible. They are living Beings with whom we communicate and who communicate with us, help us, guide us, and protect us throughout our lives in preparation for the next.

These are no glib words; but a true reality for some people today.

Others, however, believe in God alright, but He is a little distant. Sitting somewhere up there in the clouds, on His throne, looking at us, and ready to help us when we ask Him. They go to church alright, but to them at least, their relationship with their maker is not a close one. Full of reverence, of course, and perhaps tinged with a modicum of fear.

Our grandparents' sermons were full of God's wrath, fire and brimstone, and the dread of eternal damnation in hell.

But today, a sermon like that would not go down too well – would it? It would probably not be taken too seriously by church attendants, never mind those who don't go to church.

So how do we communicate God, Jesus, Heaven and hell in today's sophisticated modern world full of cynicism, bitterness and bile?

Some describe hell as being in the complete absence of God for eternity. But then, there are those in this state right now, in this very lifetime; so how can they see or understand the concept of hell, never mind fear it?

Perhaps one way is to accentuate the positive in a personal and close relationship with God. Not then … in Heaven … sometime in the future.

But here and now, today, and every day.

Through the Holy Spirit. The third Person in the Holy Trinity. The Gift. As described by St Hilary of Poitiers, (Bishop in the 3rd Century AD). Sent to us by Jesus after He was raised to Heaven.

Not much is said about the Holy Spirit in church these days.

Yet He is here, living, loving, and ready to guide us in this life, in preparation for an eternity with God, in the next.

If we let Him.

And these are no glib words either ... but meant quite literally.

GOD IN THE OLD AND NEW TESTAMENT

In the Old Testament we read about God often being full of wrath and anger sending floods everywhere and pestilence on the people and all sorts of bad things happening to those who did not tow the line. One would think He behaved like a right monster at times, thumping people on the head if they did not obey Him.

Yet in the New Testament we're told He's a loving, caring, forgiving Father who has our best interests at heart.

It does seem like a change of strategy. Does it not?

A total change of tactics from anger and wrath, and vengeance is mine, and I am a jealous God to loving one another and forgiveness.

On the face of it, it does appear that there's a great contrast between the description of God in the Old Testament and the description in the New Testament.

So let's analyze this a bit further.

We tend to see God from our human perspective. We see Him with human understanding and we attribute to Him human qualities, plans, strategies, emotions and so on.

But God is God. And man is man. We cannot possibly understand Him from our viewpoint, nor should we attempt to do so.

It could well be that the people at the time of the Old Testament were accustomed to being led, being guided, and told what to do.

See for example how Moses guided a multitude of people out of Egypt, promising them a better life elsewhere, and they all followed him willingly, even though they went round in circles in the desert for forty years

This wouldn't happen today.

In modern times people would debate Moses' proposition. They would set up committees to discuss the project, appoint several managers to chair sub-committees and devise multiple budgetary plans and operational strategies on how they would undertake the journey. I jest of course, but you get the picture.

So it could well be that God treated people in the Old Testament days the way they expected to be lead and the way they understood. With firmness where necessary, yet at all times with fairness and compassion.

Then, it could be that in His own time, according to His will, (and when we were ready for it), God eventually decided to send Jesus to us in human form to teach us, to show us God's infinite love, and to forgive and redeem us through His death and Resurrection. Jesus in human form had to be kind, gentle and compassionate to portray God's infinite love. Just as He taught us in the Lord's Prayer about a loving caring Father always ready to provide for us.

It would have been pointless to have a ruthless commanding Jesus forcing people to obey Him. This does not depict God's love for us, which is so infinite, that He gave up His own Son to die for us.

Hence the contrast between the Old and New Testaments.

Something to think about.

WOULD YOU ADAM AND EVE IT?

The reading in church was about Adam and Eve and their first sin which, allegedly, started it all.

I noticed, not for the first time I might add, that they did not in fact eat from an apple tree. No where in the story does it say what tree it was. It could have been my favourite mango fruit, or pineapples perhaps, or a variety of other fruits. All it says is that it was a fruit tree.

Which led me to think: would they have been tempted if it was a broccoli tree?

Yes I know broccoli is not a tree. Don't side track me. I was only thinking and I don't claim to always think logically.

As I was saying before you interrupted me.

Adam and Eve ate from the forbidden tree and committed their first sin.

Now a lot of us consider this to be the sin of disobedience; which in fact it was. But this is not the most serious sin which they committed.

Their major sin was that they wanted to be like God. That's what the snake (devil) had fooled them into believing. They will be like God. They will know good from bad.

To some extent that's what happened. They got to know good from bad, right from wrong, and suffered the consequences.

I suspect that these days there are many who do not really know right from wrong; or choose not to care. But that's another story.

What is important about the Adam and Eve story is how it affects us in our lives.

How often do we also try to act like gods? And want things our way?

If only I could get that job, or that promotion at work, or get so and so to love me...

Why can't other people see it my way? And do as I say? I know I'm right and people should obey me...

Dear God, Thy will be done as long as it is what I want...

Please do this, or let me have that...

Do any of these scenarios sound familiar to you? It's surprising how many people there are wishing to serve God in an advisory capacity.

We say we believe in Him and yet we tell Him, often, what to do. Rather than trust Him to know better the difference between our wants and our needs.

This does not mean that we should not pray to God and ask Him for things. Christ encouraged us to do so in the Lord's Prayer. And as a loving Father, God likes to hear our prayers and respond, sometimes, to our requests.

But let our requests be for our needs, not wants. And let us have the humility to understand that sometimes He may say "No" or "Not now ... I have something better for you!"

Let God be God. And let us be His trusting children.

He did not ask us to understand Him. Only to love and trust Him.

WHAT ARE YOU DOING NOW?

I was travelling on the train the other day. I settled down in my seat and made myself comfortable for the long journey ahead. Opposite me sat a man in his late fifties reading a newspaper. Just as the train was pulling out of the station another man entered our carriage hurriedly. The man sitting opposite looked up and recognized him immediately.

"Hello Jack ...." he greeted the newcomer, "haven't seen you for ages ... not since college days ..."

They sat together opposite me and went on for ages reminiscing about the past. I closed my eyes and hoped that the journey would soon be over. The original man sitting opposite went on to explain how he'd become Marketing Director of a large multinational firm, then he moved on elsewhere as Head of Sales and Marketing, and then as Head of this and that ... The list went on as he boasted on how well he'd done in life.

His friend had become a teacher. He joined a local school after leaving college and he'd been there ever since. He listened attentively at the long list of successes which his companion related and then asked him: "What are you doing now?"

The first man stopped in his tracks, swallowed deeply and admitted that he was out of work. He'd just attended an interview for a job in the City, but did not hold much hope.

I suppose life isn't always easy and smooth for most of us. We all have our ups and downs. Yet, no matter what we did or who we were in the past; surely what is important is what we are doing right now.

We may be at work, in between jobs, or perhaps with no job at all. The important thing is to do something right now. The past is behind us and gone. Sure, we can learn from it and use our experience to shape our future as best we can. But there really is no point in dwelling on how successful we were then.

It's not where you've been that matters. It's where you're going to!

AT HEAVEN'S DOORSTEP

I stood at the doorsteps of Heaven in full anticipation. It was not a large Pearly Gate shining brightly as we've often been told and is depicted in some pictures; no ... this was just a small wooden door. A humble ordinary wooden door with no sign or any distinguishing features foretelling where it led to.

I remembered the quote from the Bible: "Knock and it shall be opened to you ..."

I knocked and as my luck would have it the door opened outwards and hit me in the face.

An old bearded man stood there and asked: "Yes ... what do you want?"

"I ... I ... want to enter Heaven ..." I mumbled hesitantly.

"Why?" he asked abruptly.

"Because I want to spend eternity with God," I replied still fumbling for suitable words.

"And what makes you think He wants to spend an eternity with you?" retorted St Peter sternly.

It was a good question. We often assume that because we're good Christians our entry to Heaven is guaranteed, but are we judging ourselves by our standards or God's standards? I may believe that I am good to enter Heaven; but am I really?

The Saint noticed my discomfort and asked: "Who are you anyway?"

I gave him my name and he produced an electronic tablet and started punching his finger on the screen. I thought he was quite an up-to-date Saint technologically speaking considering his age.

"Ah yes … your name's here," he said finally, "I had to check. You'd be surprised how many people we get here expecting to enter Heaven as if it were a hotel. It isn't an open house for all and sundry, you know. Just because some people attended church on Sunday and did not eat meat on Friday does not automatically give them free access to Heaven.

"As my friend Matthew quoting Jesus wrote: 'Not everyone who calls me 'Lord, Lord' will enter the Kingdom of Heaven, but only those who do what my Father in Heaven wants them to do.'

"Look it up in Matthew's Gospel at 7:21.

"He always had an affectation of numbering every sentence he wrote, old Matthew did. But don't tell him I said so!"

I smiled feebly not knowing what to say.

The Saint continued: "The trouble with the world today is that too many people do the bare minimum and expect they are in God's good book. Over the years they have interpreted the Ten Commandments to be ten suggestions and debating points to discuss and amend as they wish to suit their selfish lifestyles.

"The reason God asked Moses to write them in stone is so that they don't get altered. Admittedly, Moses broke the first set; but fortunately there was another copy available.

"Over the years people have broken every Commandment even though they were set in stone.

"As I was saying to some of the disciples over tea this morning … people these days are no different to the Pharisees and Sadducees of my time on earth."

I could see Saint Peter was rather upset which was indicative to what we'd learnt about him in the Gospels. Sometimes outspoken and short-tempered. For he it was who hit a priest's servant with a sword when Jesus was arrested. I stepped slightly backwards in case he hit me with his electronic tablet.

He looked at me and chuckled, "I see here that you're due a short spell at the Purification Center" he said, "Some of you lot call it Purgatory … it's a bit like a car wash where you're cleaned up and made ready to enter Heaven for eternity. I'll be seeing you again shortly!"

I woke up with a smile on my face.

THE BALL OF WOOL

Once upon a time there was a little boy of about ten going home from school. As he crossed through the woods he met an old lady who stopped and talked to him. He told her that he was sad because he was unhappy at school. She gave him a gift of a ball of wool.

"Whenever you're unhappy" she said, "just unwind some of this wool and your unhappiness will pass away!"

For a few days he did nothing with his new gift. But one day he got home really upset because he was being bullied by the other children. He took out the ball of wool and unwound it a few turns to see what would happen.

Suddenly, he was a couple of years older, still at the same school, but no longer bullied.

He was a young teenager now, enjoying school, but he wished he could stay out late in the evenings and at weekends with his friends. His parents would not let him do so however out of love and parental caring.

"If only I was a bit older" he thought, "then my parents would allow me to go out whenever I want!"

He unwound a few more turns of the ball of wool and he was soon nineteen years old; a young man able to drive and go out with friends.

He got to like a particular young lady he met at college and wished they could date. But he was still a student, he did not have a steady job and money to buy her all the gifts he thought she deserved; and go on holidays together and enjoy themselves.

A few more turns of the ball of wool and he was in his late twenties.

Married to the girl of his dreams and with a young family. A good job and a beautiful house.

But the young children were a bit of a problem. The baby up all night, the older toddler wanting to play all the time, teething problems, childhood sickness, and all the difficulties one has with a young family that obscured his real happiness and joy. He was always tired in the mornings not having slept all night because of the baby crying. His wife tried her best to raise the family and keep home, but somehow life was difficult for all of them with all the chores one has to do.

"If only the children were a bit older" he thought; and a few more turns of the ball of wool and the kids were about eleven and nine. But sadly at this time his father became very ill and died.

The young man was totally distraught and could not get over his father's death. He lost all interest in family, work, and life in general.

"Make the pain go away" he cried as he unwound a few more turns of the ball of wool.

The children were much older now and studying at University. His hairs had gone grey a little and he struggled to go to work every day, having to drive long distances and cope with ever increasing responsibilities. He also suffered from a few minor pains and aches one gets as one gets older. His mother had grown older too and was frequently unwell. As a good son he often took her to the doctor's and for frequent hospital visits. This added to his ever increasing workload.

He felt sorry for his mother in old age, he felt sorry for his wife also getting older and struggling a little with daily life, he worried about his children having left the nest and taking their first steps into adult life. He became concerned as to how much longer he could keep working with his many ailments.

He unwound the ball of wool a little more to get out of his melancholy.

As he did so, his mother grew ever so older and eventually died.

This tragedy broke his heart more than losing his father. His children had grown up and moved away with families of their own. His wife was grey haired too and ever lovingly by his side. His minor pains and aches had developed into painful ailments and illnesses requiring constant care and medication. It was now his turn to visit doctors and hospitals for frequent check-ups.

He became ever so sad at having lost his parents; and children so far away from home that he rarely saw them. He longed to be with his grandchildren but they lived so far that he could not manage the travelling involved.

Every day became a struggle as he stayed at home nursing his many ailments and being looked after by his loving wife. He regretted his state of affairs and the fact that life could not be better.

One night, sitting in his room, he held the ball of wool now no bigger than his thumb in his trembling weak hands, and wondered where all the years had gone. He cursed the old lady who gave it to him as a gift all that long ago.

In his tiredness he fell asleep and the ball of wool fell to the ground and unwound itself completely. With a last gasp of breath he died.

The little boy of ten had lived all his life in a matter of weeks.

MORAL OF THE STORY

Know when you are really happy and thank God for it.

THE DEVIL

The devil appeared at the local supermarket one Saturday morning. He stood there by the main entrance looking menacingly and threatening. All the shoppers panicked. They escaped through every available emergency exits, jumped into their cars and drove off at speed.

All except for one shopper. A small, short man, standing there by his shopping trolley holding a long shopping list in his hand.

The devil advanced towards the small man and said angrily: "Do you know who I am?"

"Yes ... I do" replied the shopper.

"Aren't you afraid of me like all the others?" asked the devil.

"No, I've been married to your sister for 25 years!"

The devil of course is no laughing matter. He exists alright, although his greatest trick is to convince us otherwise. If you were to ask people in the street what do they know about the devil, they would probably tell you about satanic worship, or Satan possessing people, as they may have seen in the cinema. Some may mention a man with horns, a tail and pitchfork. But few would tell you of his very real existence and presence here and now.

We Christians cannot possibly believe in God and not believe in the devil or hell.

When I was at school, years ago, a schoolboy described hell as being upside-down for eternity in a pile of manure. Now, there's an image you'd probably never thought of.

Whatever you conceive it to be, hell does exist all right! It may be an ever-burning everlasting fire mixed with the acrid smell of burning flesh and sulphur. Or it may just be a state of consciousness in the total absence of God's presence and love.

And as sure as hell exists we can be certain that the devil exists too. He is not just a euphemism for evil, wickedness and wrong-doings. He is a living being, a spirit, present with us here and now, every day, and intent on the destruction of souls. He doesn't appear menacingly as he did in the supermarket in our opening story.

He is more subtle than that. He is present in our most innocent and slightest temptation; when we least expect him. He is that extra bar of chocolate we indulge in, that extra bottle of beer or glass of wine, that cigarette or whatever other weakness we may have.

He is that tiredness and sleepiness on Sunday morning which tells you it does not matter if you miss Mass this week.

He is those extra minutes you take for lunch instead of being back at work on time; or the leaving early to go home.

He is the odd flirtatious smile, which in time may lead you further on.

His subtleness and ingenuity are worthy of high praise indeed; for he tempts you when you least expect it; and the more devout you are the harder he works to get you off track.

He did after all try to tempt Christ, so you should not be much of a match for him.

Sadly for us, and fortunately for him, he has been cleverly air-brushed away from our sermons and our churches and our lives.

When is the last time you heard a sermon on Sunday about the dangers of the devil? I haven't for at least a lifetime! Yet, he belongs to the priest's sermon as surely as God does.

I wonder … Are there millions of Christians everywhere sleep-walking their way into hell?

HEAVENLY VERDICT

A man dies and goes to Heaven.

He is surprised to be lead into a well-furnished room where St Peter is sitting at a large desk in front of a computer.

St Peter invites him to sit down and taps his details into the computer.

"I'm surprised to see a computer here," says the man hesitantly, trying to make polite conversation, "I thought you'd have a big book with parchment paper and all our names written there."

"Oh … that's a common misconception," replies St Peter, "we replaced the big books years ago. They were a bit unwieldy and heavy; and they were a bit slow to use. You know what it's like … searching pages after pages for someone's name!"

"Yes," says the man nervously, "computers are much faster."

"They sure are," smiles St Peter clicking away on the keyboard, "a few key strokes here and there and we have all the information we need on view … the whole of one's life is here for me to read."

"Does the computer ever go wrong?" asks the man, sweating a little with concern about his prospects of entry, "I know they often went wrong on earth."

"Oh yes," replies the Saint chuckling quietly, "computers are computers whether on earth or here in Heaven. It's just a machine … and all machines go wrong now and then. Not like a book … what is written there remains there … unless it is altered or the page is torn away … which is obvious to the eye. You can easily see an alteration in a book.

"But computers sometimes freeze up … or play up every now and then and you can't move forward to the next screen.

"Thumping the computer on the side with an old fish I caught recently doesn't always work. I find that Control Alt and Delete does the trick but only sometimes. Either that, or I just switch it off and on again … ha ha ha … that sorts it all right! Don't try hitting the computer with something hard like a tin of sardines though. It really hurts if you get your fingers caught!" The Saint chuckled uncontrollably.

A few moments later St Peter stops chuckling to himself for a while and starts scratching his long white beard before deciding what to input next on his computer.

"But … but … what if the database is wrong? An input error somewhere in the system?" splutters the man in a panic, "you could send a poor soul in the wrong place by mistake!"

"No one goes to hell by mistake … that never happens," said the Saint confidently, "we have a fail safe system for that.

"God is supervising every transaction in another room. He has a monitor on His desk and He automatically checks every decision I make here on my computer. He is good that way … and He NEVER makes mistakes!!!

"The other day I had a guy here who had been a good man all his life. Never broke the law, was faithful to his wife, loved his children, worked hard … that sort of thing … he even went to church now and then.

"But he'd only done one good thing in his entire life … he once gave ten cents to a beggar in the street.

"I didn't know what to decide; so I emailed God. A few seconds later He replied:

" 'Give him his ten cents back and tell him to go to hell!'

"You see; God is very wise. No one goes to hell by mistake. He doesn't send anyone to hell really. It is people with their own actions who send themselves to hell."

Moral of the story:

"Not everyone who calls me 'Lord, Lord' will enter the Kingdom of Heaven, but only those who do what my Father in Heaven wants them to do." Matthew 7:21

HELLO SINNERS

Hello Sinners ... how are you?

I've often wondered; if I held a Sinners Convention how many people would turn up? Not many I suppose and I'd lose a lot of money hiring the venue and having refreshments ready.

The reason I suppose is because most of us don't consider ourselves to be sinners. Not big ones anyway. For the most part, we all believe we're good people deep down and we will eventually go to Heaven, because we're good really! It's all a matter of time.

I mean ... when is the last time you killed someone?

Or robbed a bank?

Or embezzled from your employer or business?

Or coveted your neighbour's wife/husband, or ass? (I must admit I'm very envious of my neighbour's roses. Why does he grow better flowers than me?)

OK ... I know ... some people do cheat on their partners and think nothing of it. It's their right to be happy in life is it not? (Or so they think!)

And that's where the problem lies ... "or so they think".

Many people believe that a slight flirtation or infidelity is OK. They think that having a fixation on materialism is harmless really. What's wrong with having a big house, car, plenty of jewelry or whatever? What's wrong with gossiping and telling tales about other people?

It's harmless fun really.

So what if they don't have time to look after elderly parents living alone? They live too far anyway, and life is busy these days with work, looking after the kids and so on.

Don't tell me that taking the odd bit of stationery home from work is wrong. It's not stealing is it? Not like robbing a bank. And what's wrong with having a long lunch hour? Or getting to work late or leaving early? Really!

Anyway ... these are all small sins, if sins at all. Not like killing and really stealing and the other sins mentioned in the Ten Commandments.

It's this kind of thinking, all too prevalent I suppose, which means that not many people would attend my Sinners Convention ... or so I'm told.

BUOY ... OH BUOY

Imagine you're a child taken by your parents to the beach, or the swimming pool. You've never been near so much water before. But it's time to try. Hesitantly, encouraged by a grown up, you splash water everywhere in a panic, and you hold tight to the buoy they've given you for safety.

Clever thing the buoy – a ring filled with air able to hold you up when you're drowning.

Every rescue boat has some on board and every ship is equipped with several – just in case.

But what about when we're on terra firma so to speak? When we go about our way throughout our lives.

We often encounter many dangers and difficulties, be they of our own making or they "just happen" as they often do.

Crises like sudden illness, loss of work, relationship breakdowns, financial hardships and so on. You name it; most of us have encountered it.

We panic, we splash about, we try to hold tight to someone for help – a relative, a friend, just anyone before we loose control and drown in the depth of our own personal crisis.

And as we struggle to keep our head above water we forget what we should do instinctively ... reach out to God.

A drowning man instinctively reaches out to a buoy for safety.

And so should we – instinctively, in full confidence, we should know in every crisis that He is there, ready to help.

Every hesitant minute which delays our reaching out to Him is a wasted minute drifting us away from His omnipotent presence.

Oh ... and one more thing.

When Peter got off the boat and walked towards Jesus on the waves he succeeded for a moment or two because he was focused on Christ. The moment his focus moved away to the waves and the sea he began to sink.

What's the point having a Leader who walks on water if we are not prepared to follow Him?

FRAGILE FAITH

Some people have great Faith and no matter what may befall them, their Faith does not waver. It is as strong as ever.

Other people however are different. They believe alright, but at the first sign of difficulties they hesitate, and doubts take over, and shake their Faith somewhat.

How does God view these latter people? Does He despair, as Jesus did when His disciples hesitated and could not drive out a demon from a sick child? Matthew 17: 14-21.

Let's imagine you're a parent of several children. One of them is academically gifted and does well at his studies; he is also very athletic and excels at many sports. The other child is more pedestrian; a slow learner who is neither academically gifted nor interested in much in particular.

Do you love them equally? Do you pay as much care and attention to both? Do you encourage the gifted one more than the other? Or do you nurture and look after the slower child more to help him gain confidence and improve?

God loves us all equally; yet He knows our abilities and our limitations. He knows that some of us have a fragile Faith that may well falter under pressure. Yet, like Jesus, He may well raise His eyes to Heaven in frustration, but He never stops loving us. He never stops encouraging us to do better, and increase our trust in Him. He allows incidents to happen in our lives to give us an opportunity to trust Him more and more.

It's the outright rebellious and disobedient He disapproves of – not the hesitant "tryer" who tries his best yet his weak Faith lets him down.

When we look at the disciples and the saints we see that they were not all perfect. Many of them stumbled many times along the way to Heaven. It is said that saints are sinners who never gave up trying. "I believe, Lord; help my unbelief." Mark 9:24.

HAVE YOU HEARD THE ONE ABOUT…

The comedian stood on the stage and shouted "12".

And the audience laughed in unison.

He then said "15" and they laughed even louder.

He cried out "23" and they stamped their feet with delight as they laughed and applauded.

He continued with his repertoire "24 ... 33 ... 39 ..." and the audience was in tears with laughter as he kept calling out various numbers.

After about fifteen minutes or so on stage I asked him afterwards in his room what all that was about.

He explained, "This is a very loyal audience who follow me everywhere wherever I do a show. Over the years they got to know all my jokes and they enjoy hearing them over and again. In order to make the show go faster, and so that I can pack in more jokes, I have printed them all out and numbered them. The audience has memorized all the jokes. Now all I have to do is call out the number, they remember the joke, and laugh at it!"

I was amazed at what he had just said. "Why ..." I asked hesitantly, "why did they not laugh when you said 42?"

"They had not heard that joke before!" he answered.

Every winter we hear the story of Christmas read out in church several times. A pregnant Virgin and her husband go to Bethlehem on a donkey. There is no room in the inn. They go to the stable where a baby is born and placed in a manger. An Angel appears to shepherds and announces the Birth; and a star guides three Kings from the East to the stable.

We've all heard the story many times before and no doubt we will hear it again next Christmas and beyond.

Is it yet another old story from folklore which tradition repeats every twelve months and, like that comedian's audience, we remember once again and smile silently as we celebrate with family and friends?

Or is it perhaps something more important than that? In fact, the most important event that has ever happened in the history of the world.

God, the Creator of the whole Universe and what is in it and beyond it, loved us so much that He decided to make Himself flesh and visit us on earth as a human being.

I wonder how many people, as they celebrate the "12" days of Christmas from the 25th to the 6th, stop for a moment and really and seriously think about the awesomeness that this event really means?

1? ... 3? ... 7? ... 100? ... More?

MESSAGES

Isn't it annoying when you're waiting for an important letter and the postman never comes. Or he delivers a lot of bills and adverts but not the letter you want.

I accept that sometimes he has no letters for me. When that is the case, why can't he ring the door bell and tell me he has no letters for me?

After all, when I check my computer it tells me there are no new messages on the server. So why can't the postman?

And why doesn't God say to the world "I have no new messages for you. The message is the same as it ever was. I love you so much that I sacrificed my only Son, Jesus, for you." (John 3:16).

The devil on the other hand, well … he's always got new messages for us. New temptations. New ways to lead us astray. New ways to rebel against God.

Or is it perhaps that God is telling us daily His Good News of our salvation, by His Grace, through Jesus – and we're just not listening.

Now here's a thought!

THE LEANING TREE

Father Francis Maple in one of his sermons makes a good point about our relationship with God by referring to a leaning tree. Here's what he says:

I think of a life as a tree. If a tree leans in one direction when it dies it will fall in that direction. It is not going to fall in the opposite direction. So, too, with our lives. If all the time we are leaning towards God, very likely, with God's grace we shall fall into His arms when we die. But if our lives never point to God, it is very likely that when we die we shall die in enmity with God.

Father Francis Maple

GOD'S INVITATION

Someone asked me whether God wants everyone to come to Him, and, since He knows everything, if anyone refuses to follow God's Word, then did this man really have a choice, or was it pre-determined that he would not follow God.

Pre-determination and free will have been debated by Christians and non-Christians for years.

Here's my view on it.

God's invitation is to everyone - without exception. When He invites us to love Him, He wants us to choose freely - without any pressure on His part to influence our decision. We choose to love Him and come to God through Jesus Christ: "I am the way, the truth, and the life; no one goes to the Father except by me." John 14:6.

Of course, some choose not to accept the invitation. They decide to walk away from God. Not to believe in Him and in Jesus as His only Son. That is their free choice.

God in His infinite wisdom knows our decision before we even make it - but He does not influence it in any way. He knows that some people will not believe in Him.

In certain cases He allows this to happen.

It's like you being in a helicopter watching two cars coming at an intersection. You know they will hit each other. Yet you do not influence or change the outcome.

There are times however when God does try to influence our decision. Give us a nudge in the right direction, you might say.

Note that I say "influence" and not force our decision.

Why He does that in only some cases we really don't know.

A well known example of His influence is the manner He "encouraged" Paul on the way to Damascus. I suppose Paul could still have walked away and not followed God's Word; although I doubt many would have done so under the circumstances! Paul chose to accept God and the rest, as they say, is history.

Today God does nudge some of us in the right direction. How?

Perhaps through chance meetings with someone who might talk to us about God and encourage us to accept His Word and take up His invitation to love Him. Maybe He allows certain things to happen in our lives which make us turn to Him.

But the fact is that He does talk to us. He does invite us to come to Him through Jesus Christ. Perhaps some of us just aren't listening.

And here's the important distinction to remember. God tries to encourage us to accept His Word.

But He never forces us. We are free to choose to love Him, or not.

ADULTERY

Once upon a time there was a priest who got fed up with the number of parishioners who confessed that they committed adultery. Every week, in the confessional, it was the same thing - adultery.

One Sunday he said in his sermon that he was angry about this continuous sin of adultery amongst his congregation. He promised that if he heard this sin one more time he'd give up the priesthood and leave town for ever.

His congregation loved him and did not want to lose him. They agreed a secret code amongst themselves. From now on, instead of saying they committed adultery; they would say they have "fallen".

All went well for years until eventually the bishop moved the priest to another Parish and replaced him with a new one.

The new priest did not know the code. He was most disturbed that so many parishioners kept falling so he complained to the Mayor that the sidewalks in town were un-even and that he should do something about it to stop people from falling.

The Mayor, knowing the code, laughed out loudly.

The priest said: "I don't know what you're laughing about. Your wife fell three times this week."

Do you remember when the Pharisees brought to Jesus a woman caught committing adultery?

According to Jewish law she had to be stoned to death for that sin.

We're told in the Gospel of John that Jesus wrote in the sand with His finger. We're not told what He wrote. I guess He wrote 'Dear God ... will they never learn?'

But that's not important; what is important is that after He said let the one who has never sinned throw the first stone, and when they all left one by one, Jesus turned to the woman and asked 'Is there no one left to condemn you?'

She said 'No one ...'

Jesus replied 'I do not condemn you either. Go, but do not sin again.'

Now Jesus did not mean do not sin any sin whatsoever ever again for the rest of your life!

He knew that that would be impossible. The woman was human, and it is natural that she would sin again. Jesus knows our human nature and He knows that we are liable to sin again and again.

What Jesus said to the woman is, do not commit that particular sin again. It is serious enough to get you into a lot of trouble with the Pharisees as well as with God Himself.

And that's what Jesus is saying to us today.

He knows we are weak. He knows that we will sin; which is why we have the Holy Sacrament of Confession.

By saying 'do not sin again' Jesus is warning us to beware of those particular sins which are serious enough to lead us into damnation, and into an eternity of exclusion from our Father in Heaven.

As we prepare for our weekly confession we need to consider carefully the seriousness of our sins. Which ones are venial sins; and which ones are grave enough to exclude us from God's ever lasting love.

In our propensity to sin, God is loving and caring enough to forgive us again and again.

But with our confession there should also be remorse and guilt for what we have done. Confession should not be just a laborious recitation of the same old sins; and a futile exercise which serves no one and certainly does not fool God Himself.

Without true remorse, and a genuine resolve not to repeat our sins; then confession means nothing. And it would be better not to go to confession at all. At least that is honest in the eyes of God.

TEACHING ABOUT GOD

The preacher was telling the congregation about the evils of drink. "To drink is to follow Satan. Drink is bad for you. It will lead you to damnation".

To demonstrate his point he put two glasses on the pulpit. One contained water and one contained whisky. He then produced a small box containing two worms which he had dug from the garden before the service began.

He placed a worm in the glass of water and it floated about merrily. He then put the second worm in the glass of whisky and after wriggling for a few seconds it died.

"What does this tell you?" he asked.

A member of the congregation replied, "If you have worms drink whisky".

There's a message in this joke for us Christians. How often, whilst well-meaning, we try to tell others about our beliefs and end up confusing them and perhaps, un-wittingly, driving them away from God rather than towards Him.

It is worth remembering that not everyone is at the same stage of knowing God as perhaps we are. You wouldn't feed a new-born baby pizza or French fries; would you? So let's go easy with new Christians or people who have yet to know the Lord as we do.

The best way to teach Christianity is by living it as Jesus would want us to.

"Preach the Gospel at all times and when necessary use words."
St Francis of Assisi.

SILENT PRAYER

In a Catholic Church, when we celebrate Mass, just before the Gospel is read, the congregation makes a small Sign of the Cross on their forehead, on their lips, and on their breast.

What's all that about?

In fact, it is a silent prayer all by itself.

The Sign of the Cross on one's forehead reminds us that the Word of God should always be in the forefront of our minds. No matter what we do throughout life, it should always be in accordance to God's wishes and God's Commandments. By keeping God always on our mind we ensure that we're always close to Him and that we're less likely to go against His will.

The Sign on our lips means that we pray that we're always prepared to witness for God when the right time requires it. Many people often shy away from speaking up for God in conversation with family and friends, especially when He is ridiculed or spoken against. People tend to keep quiet for fear of offending others, or for fear of being ridiculed themselves. Instead, our lips can often be used to gossip, malign others, to spread rumours, lies and ill will. The Sign on our lips is a prayer that our lips are always used to glorify and serve God in all that we say.

The Sign on our breast is a prayer that God may always be within our heart and that we may grow to love Him and never stray from His love. Hearts can often hide grudges, hatred, revenge, envy, and all sorts of other sins. Signing the Cross on our heart is a prayer that we may be always pure and receptive to God's love and grace.

The Sign of the Cross on our forehead, lips and hearts. A silent prayer all in itself.

KYRIE ELEISON

Originally, the Mass in Eastern Europe, where it started, was celebrated in Greek.

With time, as Christianity spread further West into Europe it was celebrated in Latin.

And as time moved on, it is now celebrated in English, or whichever language is spoken in the Country where Mass is celebrated.

Except for three words which have survived time and are still from the original Greek Mass.

Kyrie Eleison
Christe Eleison

Meaning "Lord have mercy" and "Christ have mercy".

It is important to remember that by "Lord", or "Sir" we do not mean that we look up to Our Lord as some Master or Ruler. In this context, the word "Kyrie" means "Lord" in the sense of a child looking up to one's loving parent and asking for help, love, guidance and protection.

So when we sing at Mass "Kyrie Eleison" we look up to God our loving Father and ask Him to be always by our side and have mercy on us. And we call upon Christ His Son, in the same prayer.

ALLELUIA

When celebrating a Catholic Mass, just before the reading of the Gospel, the congregation and choir sing "Alleluia". It's an old English word, derived from Latin, and originally from the Hebrew word Halleluyah meaning "Praise the Lord!"

Now ... if we look carefully in our Missal, it says "May be omitted if not sung". Have you ever wondered why it says so?

Well ... let's imagine you are at a Birthday Party and in a straight face you recite calmly:

Happy Birthday to you
Happy Birthday to you
Happy Birthday dear friend
Happy Birthday to you

It doesn't quite have the same effect does it? It just has to be sung.

Some songs have to be sung. They cannot be recited, however well we might try.

And it's the same with the "Alleluia". It is an ancient song of praise to Our Lord giving us all an opportunity, however bad we may think our voices are, to praise Our Lord in song for all He has done for us.

So let us raise our voices in joy and Praise Him now and when we next attend Mass.

THE LORD'S PRAYER

"Our Father who art in heaven ..."

"Yes. How can I help you?"

"Hein? Who's that?"

"You called me. I'm listening ..."

"I didn't call anybody ... I was just praying ... The Lord's Prayer! Our Father who art in Heaven ..."

"That's me ... Your Father in Heaven ... now carry on praying ..."

"Eh ... Hallowed be Thy name ..."

"Ha ... Do you remember when you were very young you used to say 'Harold be Thy name'? For a long time you were convinced my name is Harold; until someone put you right. What does it mean anyway ... Hallowed be Thy name?"

"Eh ... hmmm ... does it mean you are Holy?"

"That's right ... carry on ..."

"Thy kingdom come, Thy will be done, on earth as it is in Heaven."

"Hold it just there ... Do you really mean what you just said?"

"Sure, of course I do ..."

"Or do you mean 'Thy will be done' as long as it is what you want? Do you really accept my will all the time? Even when it's not convenient for you, or when life gets a little difficult?"

"Well ... sometimes when things get really bad I get very worried."

"At least you're honest. Remember this always; when things are really bad for you it is still my will. I allow it to happen but I never abandon you. I'm always close to you … all you have to do is trust me."

"Gee … thanks."

"Carry on …"

"Give us this day our daily bread …"

"Let's stop again … This means that I will provide for all your needs. It's good of you to ask; but rest assured that I will always provide you with what you need. Go on with your prayer."

"Forgive us our trespasses as we forgive those who trespass against us …"

"Even your neighbour?"

"What?"

"You never forgave your neighbour after that argument you had a few days ago … In fact you still hope that you'll get even some day."

"But … but … You know it was his fault!"

"Of course it was … and he did apologize. But unless you truly forgive him, you truly no longer hold a grudge and have no ill-will or ill-feelings towards him; it doesn't count does it?"

"That's not always easy …"

"I agree … But true forgiveness means that you no longer wish any retribution or revenge against those who have hurt you. Sure … you'll always remember the wrong done to you, but let that be a reminder to forgive them once again and to pray for them."

"Can I go on now?"

"Yes …"

"And lead us not into temptation. But deliver us from evil."

"This bit is a reminder that Satan is always there trying to take you away from me. He tried to tempt my only Son Jesus, so you're not going to be much of a challenge to him. Whenever he tries to lead you astray repeat those words over and again and I will come to your help."

"Thank you …"

"It's getting late … go to sleep now!"

MONEY MONEY MONEY

I'm sure you know the story about the rich man who was told by Jesus to sell everything he had, give it to the poor, and follow Jesus. Mark 10:17-27.

The man just could not do this, and went away sad.

Jesus also says that famous saying about it being harder for a rich man to enter Heaven than for a camel to go through the eye of a needle.

And people have been debating that hyperbole for years. What did it mean? Did Jesus refer to a gate called Needle, or was it a mountain pass which was so narrow you had to unload your camel of what it was carrying, pass the camel through, and then load it again?

In reality, it doesn't matter.

What's important is the message behind the hyperbole and the advice to sell everything and give it to the poor.

Did Jesus mean it?

Here's my take on it – unorthodox as it may be.

I doubt very much if every rich man on earth sold all their property and gave it to the poor that it would make any difference. It would be like putting a snowflake in a burning furnace.

Anyway, it is not physically possible, since if every rich person sold their property, by implication, they would sell it to someone else who would in turn be rich in order to be able to buy it. I'm sure you follow the tautology.

So what did Jesus mean?

He certainly was not speaking against wealth. Wealth creates wealth. It creates jobs and it creates the wherewithal to help others less fortunate than ourselves.

Christ condones, nay encourages, the creation of wealth in His parable about the servants given a gold coin each by their master. When he returned from his travels the master discovered that two servants managed to make their fortune increase whilst the third just didn't bother. So he rewards the hard-working servants and punishes the other. Luke 19:11-27.

Jesus was teaching responsible wealth. There's nothing wrong in working hard and amassing a fortune honestly.

As long as we use it responsibly.

Those who are fortunate to have wealth should remember their responsibility to share it with others, and to help others, as best they can. This doesn't mean sell everything and give it to the poor. It means be aware of those around you who are less fortunate than yourself; and share your good fortune with them.

If you were to sell everything then once it's gone, it's gone - you can no longer help the poor and you may well become poor yourself. What's so clever about that?

In the parable of the rich man and Lazarus (Luke 16:19-31) Jesus does not condemn the rich man for being rich; but for not even realizing, never mind caring, for a poor man starving at his gate.

So there you have it: work hard, be wealthy, but remember others less well-off than yourself.

And wealth does not necessarily mean riches and money.

Some people are wealthy in different ways: wealthy in wisdom and knowledge, wealthy in health and stamina, wealthy in talents and so on.

Those amongst us who are well educated and knowledgeable should not look down on others haughtily and with disdain. Use your knowledge to teach others.

Those who are fortunate to be healthy should remember the sick and if possible visit them or help them as best they can.

Those with talents for music, the arts, sports or whatever, should share their talents with others. Imagine the good you can achieve as a sportsman if you visit a school and share a few moments coaching children in whatever it is you do. Or if a musician or celebrity shared a few moments with less talented yet aspiring youngsters. That visit would be imprinted on young memories for life – and may well inspire them to do better and achieve more.

Let's all look at ourselves deeply and discover what wealth God has given us.

Money, good health, a talent for music, painting, singing or whatever … and let's share it for the glory of, and in thanksgiving to, God our Creator.

HOW IMPORTANT ARE YOU?

How important are you? Really?

Who are you exactly?

Wife? Husband? Parent? Daughter? Son? Sister? Brother? Friend?

Married? Single? Divorced? Widowed?

What do you do in life?

Home-maker? Home-schooling? Self-employed? Employee?

Lawyer? Doctor? Mechanic? Carpenter?

How many people rely on you in life?

Your spouse and children? Elderly parents and siblings? Colleagues at work? Neighbours and friends?

What do you do for them in life? Nurture your family who rely on you as your dependents? Help your parents with chores they can no longer do for themselves? Or be there for them as their health fails them? Be there for your family, siblings, colleagues and friends when they need you?

Perhaps you also help an elderly neighbour with the shopping, or gardening or other chores. Or you may visit people in hospital or in prison or provide food and clothing for the down-and-out in the streets?

Maybe you help in church with the cleaning, writing the newsletter, playing the organ or a member of the choir? Or be more active on the Parish Council or whatever else is needed to be done in church.

You know ... even the dog and cat rely on you for food and shelter!

Just think for a moment how many people rely on you and whose lives you have touched by just being here right now. And how their lives would be affected if you were no longer here.

How important are you?

Very important, I should say. A VIP no less.

Think of that next time you pray. And ask God to look after YOU.

Not for your sake; but for the sake of all others who rely on you.

SORRY

Is saying "Sorry" the hardest word?

As human beings, it is inevitable that we will make mistakes and that unintentionally we will hurt others. So it follows that we should apologize when we err, and that we are forgiven our sins.

Yet, in this modern world of ours we hesitate before we admit our wrong-doings.

We see an apology as a sign of weakness. It would reveal a flaw in our character. Something to be held against us, which may well come to haunt us again in the future.

We feel threatened even, since, in this litigious society we have created, an admission of guilt could easily lead to claims for compensation.

So we go on the defensive. We deny wrong-doings. We refuse to apologize.

And "sorry" truly becomes the hardest word.

How lucky we are that God does not keep a record of our sins, and will never rush to Court for compensation when we hurt Him again and again.

Peter came to Jesus and asked, "Lord, if my brother keeps sinning against me, how many times do I have to forgive him? Seven times?"

"No, not seven times," answered Jesus, "but seventy times seven." Matthew 18: 21-22

FACE TO FACE WITH ST PETER

St Peter opened the Gates of Heaven one morning to find an elderly woman waiting there.

"Ah ..." he said, "I wasn't expecting you so early. Normally guests start arriving at about mid-morning. Anyway ... what is your name?"

The woman gave her name and the old Saint put on his reading glasses and started typing on his computer. Moments later her details came up on the screen.

"Aha ... you've had a tough life I see ... I'm sorry to read all about it. You overcame many trials and tribulations and suffered many pains and heartaches."

The woman smiled feebly.

"You were generally very kind too ... and you prayed a lot. Often reciting the Rosary on your knees! I bet you have calloused knees!" he laughed.

She blushed a little and said nothing.

He tapped at the keyboard a few times and then added, "generous too, you gave to the poor as much as you could spare ..."

She looked down to the ground and said nothing.

"Oh ... Oh ..." he said with a frown, "what's this I read here? It is written in red; and underlined too.

"For almost a lifetime you have not forgiven someone ... why is that?"

She trembled a little and muttered, "That person hurt me very badly."

"That's true," said the Saint, "it says so here on my computer."

"And the hurt never went away," added the old lady trying to justify her actions, "every time I remembered I hurt once again ..."

"Yes I know," interrupted St Peter, "it says so here."

"And that person never asked for my forgiveness either," continued the old lady sensing a reprieve.

"The thing is," interrupted the Saint once again, "you never actually wanted to forgive did you? You held on to the hurt as a crutch which in time became a stick to beat that person with ... not literally, but certainly in your mind.

"Every time you remembered the hurt you felt ill-will towards that person. Even though they may not have asked for forgiveness you would not have granted forgiveness if asked. In fact their lack of asking forgiveness itself became an instrument of growth for your crutches and the stick to beat him with."

She trembled, fearing the worst, and said nothing.

"Yet ... at all times, you recited Our Lord's own words 'forgive us our trespasses as we forgive those who trespassed against us' and did not meant a word you said.

"He is very hurt by that!" admonished the Saint as gently as he could, "Our Lord has often been misquoted and this short phrase I fear is the most common misquotation of all."

At this the old lady began weeping uncontrollably.

"Our Lord, my Master, is very forgiving indeed," continued St Peter, "I know that from personal experience. Also on the Cross He forgave his oppressors. And a few days later He forgave Thomas too.

"As for the memories … of course He still has them. Every time He looks at the scars on His hands and feet, and on His side, the memories come back to Him as painful and raw as if it were yesterday. And every time He remembers, He forgives once again!"

She wiped her eyes with her veil and continued weeping.

The Saint switched off his computer and shut the Gates behind him as he re-entered Heaven.

GOD'S BLUEPRINT

I asked a Christian doctor friend of mine about his religion and his profession. He explained that being a doctor is very much like being a car mechanic. He learnt about different parts of the body and how to fix them when they go wrong.

However, unlike a car mechanic, he does not have the complete blueprint plan of how the body was made and how it functions. He explained that, thankfully, the Creator decided to keep some parts of the blueprint secret in case we humans ruin the final product completely.

What do you think?

SUFFERING

I was day dreaming the other day and I wondered; what if I came face to face with a genie? You know, the one out of a bottle or an old oil lamp. And what if he gave me one wish.

Just one wish. What would it be?

Happiness for myself and my family? Riches? Good health? That's three wishes for a start; and I only have one wish to make.

As I sobered up and considered this carefully I thought I'd ask the genie to end all suffering in the world.

Now wouldn't that be wonderful? No more suffering from hunger and poverty. No more suffering from illness and old age. No more suffering from violence and bullying. No more suffering of any kind anywhere in the world.

I wonder what that would be like.

Then I thought about suffering. It comes our way from time to time and stays with us for varying periods, sometimes for ever, and hurts us to varying degrees.

Why, and what should we do about it?

I believe that God allows suffering to come our way for reasons best known to Himself.

But I also believe that He takes no great delight in seeing us suffer. It isn't for Him a means by which He somehow "purifies" us from our sins, or an essential condition which we should accept gladly as a badge of honour, or some sort of sacrifice to repay Him for what He has done for us.

Let's face it; there is NOTHING we can do which will ever repay what God did for us. And He does not, and never has, asked for repayment by means of suffering and donning sackcloth and ashes.

In fact the New Testament is full of evidence that God is against our suffering.

Christ acted against suffering when He saw the sick and the poor, the blind, the deaf, the dumb and the lame, as well as those possessed by the devil. On every occasion He stopped suffering by healing those brought to Him. Even when suffering was the result of death itself, as for instance when His friend Lazarus died and his family were distraught; Christ acted against the suffering of death and raised Lazarus once again.

I suppose it can be said that Jesus took upon Him all the suffering of the world when He hung dying on the Cross.

And even today, Christ is fighting against suffering. For He is alive and with us now as He was after the Resurrection.

His Holy Spirit fights against suffering through the hands of many who can heal through prayers and the miracles performed in His name. His Holy Spirit is at work fighting suffering through the miracles in Lourdes and elsewhere. His Holy Spirit is fighting suffering through the miracles and intercessions of the Saints. And His Holy Spirit is fighting suffering through us; yes ... you and me.

When suffering befalls us God does not want us to accept it as a sacrifice and suffer in silence. To do so is tantamount to saying that He wills it and delights in it and we should accept it.

God does not ask the sick man to suffer in joy and not seek any medical advice, not to pray for healing and to do nothing about it; anymore than He asks anyone to accept suffering willingly and do nothing about it.

Only Christ accepted suffering willingly and He did so for a Divine purpose to redeem us all from our sins.

That God wills our suffering is in no doubt. But I repeat, He does not delight in it and He does not wish us just to accept it without any attempt to confront it and fight it. He would wish us to act against the evil of suffering just as Christ did when He walked this earth.

Through prayers we act and seek help for the ending or easing of our suffering and that of others. Through the intercession of the Saints, the Archangel Rafael known as The Healer, or through the help of those blessed with the power of healing. We can and should act to ease or end our suffering whatever it may be.

Like the woman who dared to touch Christ's garment we too should dare to ask for His help; rather than accept suffering as if it were our duty to just grin and bear it.

To suffer in silence and do nothing about it is a great disservice to the Lord as it portrays a certain lack of Faith in Him and His love and mercy.

We often hear of people who have suffered great pain and illness for years being miraculously healed. Whatever their reason for their suffering, whether it was ill health or something else, their suffering is eased or ended. On every occasion when such miracles occur it is because people have placed their Faith in God to end their situation and condition. They may have visited a Faith healer, they may have visited a shrine like Lourdes, they may have asked a Saint's or Archangel's help. But they did something, rather than accept their suffering and not confront it.

And we too, you and me, can perform our little miracles and end suffering when we see it in others.

When we see Lazarus starving at our doorstep, when we see the old neighbour needing help with the shopping or the housekeeping, when we see our colleague at work struggling under the bullying of an oppressive boss … we too can reach out our hand and help in some way to ease and end that suffering.

Maybe that is why God allows suffering to happen in the world. Not for us to accept it and suffer in silence. But to give an opportunity to others who see our conditions to help in any way they can to end or ease our suffering.

When I think about it, we don't need a genie to end the suffering of the world. We have the power of that genie within us. We just don't want to use it.

IF NOT NOW WHEN

Once upon a time there was an elderly lady who had a bone china tea set. She had a teapot, a milk jug, a container for sugar, twelve cups and saucers and side plates for biscuits and cakes. The individually hand-made items where white in colour with beautiful red roses hand-painted as decorations and gold plating on the rims of the cups and plates. Although the set was quite old it was in pristine condition as if it had just left the factory; now long closed and out of business.

She loved that tea set and displayed it proudly in a glass-fronted cupboard in her living room.

She never used it because it was reserved for very special occasions. You know, just in case the Pope or the Queen might visit. Which of course they never did; nor were they likely to ever do. The old lady was very concerned in case an item would break or be chipped in use and the set would be incomplete and the damaged item irreplaceable

The tea set remained in the glass-fronted cupboard, admired by everyone who visited the old lady, and proudly loved by her whenever she looked at it.

One day the old lady died and her distant relatives, who never visited her when alive, sold all her belongings and used the money towards a holiday abroad.

When the old lady met St Peter at the Gates of Heaven, for that is where she was destined, the old Saint, who was used to drinking from an old clay cup when on earth, remarked casually "You never did get to use that lovely tea set, did you?"

"No!" she replied forlornly, "I saved it for a special occasion which never arrived!"

"Hmmm ..." thought the Saint stroking his beard, "You also never got round to planting aubergines and courgettes in your garden. You always wanted to do that. But never did!"

"That's right …" remembered the old lady, "Somehow I never got round to it. You know how it is … I was busy cleaning the house and things."

St Peter chuckled quietly and added "Buon giorno!"

The old lady looked up at the tall man in total confusion.

He laughed and said, "Remember that winter when you promised yourself to learn Italian? You even bought a book and a dictionary, but never got to enroll at the local college for evening classes."

"Yes … that's right …" she replied shyly, "I wish I'd done that. Somehow the time was never right to start those classes. I would have enjoyed them too!"

An ominous silence followed and she wondered frightfully whether her omissions had somehow prejudiced her chances of entering Paradise.

"Do come in, my dear!" said the kindly Saint, "you know …" he added as he scratched his head, "it grieves me when I look down on earth and see so many people procrastinating and postponing doing something they set their hearts on.

"I watch and think … if not now, when?

"Somehow, people always have a reason for not doing something. When the Big Boss created the world for us He meant us to enjoy His creations, not postpone them and endure life!"

As she was led to her room in Paradise she discovered by her bedside the porcelain tea-set she once owned, two packets of aubergine and courgette seeds and an Italian dictionary.

The kindly Saint had given her a second chance to fulfill her dreams.

ARE YOU LISTENING?

There is a great difference of course between hearing and listening.

We hear the noise of the traffic outside, an airplane flying overhead or the TV in the background and we pay no attention.

But when we listen we have to concentrate, to pay attention, to understand and remember what is being said. It is difficult and tiring.

Our level of concentration depends on who is doing the talking. From a baby saying his first words, to a child seeking our attention or our spouse or boss speaking – our level of concentration and listening differs greatly.

It therefore follows that the more important to us the speaker is, and the more vital the message, the more we have to listen carefully.

And who is more important than God?

Is He speaking to you right now?

Are you listening?

LOVE … LOVE?

I was reading a letter the other day from a man named Paul to some friends of his in Corinth. Here's what he says:

"If I speak in the tongues of men and of angels, but have not love, I am only a resounding gong or a clanging cymbal. If I have the gift of prophecy and can fathom all mysteries and all knowledge, and if I have a faith that can move mountains, but have not love, I am nothing. If I give all I possess to the poor and surrender my body to the flames, but have not love, I gain nothing." 1 Corinthians 13:1-3.

Wow !!! That's powerful stuff I thought. If we have Faith to move mountains yet have not love it counts for nothing. Even if we give all we own to the poor? I'm not so sure about the burning body bit; but this man is over the top I tell you.

Let's see what Jesus has to say about this. Better go to the expert, I always say.

"Love the Lord your God with all your heart and with all your soul and with all your mind. This is the first and greatest commandment. And the second is like it: Love your neighbour as yourself." Matthew 22:37-39.

What?

Love my neighbour? Even when he's wrong?

Love the guy driving that big van this morning and keeping a distance of just three inches from the back of my car? And hooting his horn time and again even though I was driving within the speed limit? Perhaps he was in a hurry to go to the toilet!

Love that obnoxious pompous boss at work who seems to delight in making everyone suffer?

Love that guy at the pub who always knows it all; and is a pain in the neck working his way South?

Is this what Jesus says? And He goes on:

"But I tell you who hear me: Love your enemies, do good to those who hate you, bless those who curse you, pray for those who mistreat you. If someone strikes you on one cheek, turn to him the other also. If someone takes your cloak, do not stop him from taking your tunic. Give to everyone who asks you, and if anyone takes what belongs to you, do not demand it back. Do to others as you would have them do to you." Luke 6:27-31.

And there I was thinking that going to Heaven is a matter of ticking the right boxes: Baptism? Done that. Tick. Go to church on Sundays? Done that. Tick. A few more ticks here and there and my passport and visa are ready for me to enter Heaven!

On reflection, being a Christian is much more difficult than it seems at first.

"Not everyone who calls me 'Lord, Lord' will enter the Kingdom of Heaven, but only those who do what my Father in Heaven wants them to do." Matthew 7:21.

In other words – There are no parrots in Heaven.

I LOST MY BOW TIE

There I was the other day in a hurry to attend an important meeting when … dash it all … I could not find my bow tie!

You know the one; light turquoise with small pink flowers!

I looked everywhere and could not find it. Perhaps my cat had taken it and used it as a toy. It had vanished and I was in a hurry.

I prayed to St Anthony to help me find it but I think he was too busy searching for something else. So I chose my spotted ordinary tie instead, put on my best hat, and off I went.

Whilst in the taxi I thought about that old lady in the Bible who'd lost a coin. When she found it she held a party for her friends and neighbours to celebrate. Well, I certainly won't be doing that if I ever find my bow tie! Cheaper to buy another one, I thought. Although light turquoise with small pink flowers is somewhat rare, I tell you.

Then my thoughts wandered about what else people can lose and feel really bad about.

Money … jewelry … prized possessions … someone's love perhaps … or even worse, a loved one.

It must be terrible when we lose a loved one and, although we believe as Christians that people go to a better place when they die, their departure does affect us greatly. We miss them … and to miss someone means that their presence had a good effect on our lives. Now they're gone we feel the pain and anguish of their absence.

My empty brain was freewheeling now with one thought following another aimlessly through the various dark recesses of my mind.

What, for me, would be the greatest thing I could ever lose; something from which I would never recover, besides my turquoise bow tie, that is? A small voice deep into my cranium whispered: My Faith.

MISSED

Then He led them out of the city as far as Bethany, where He raised His hands and blessed them. As He was blessing them, He departed from them and was taken up into Heaven.
Luke 24:50.

After saying this, He was taken up to Heaven as they watched Him, and a cloud hid Him from their sight. They still had their eyes fixed on the sky as He went away, when two men dressed in white suddenly stood beside them and said, "Galileans, why are you standing there looking up at the sky? This Jesus, who was taken from you into Heaven, will come back in the same way that you saw Him go to Heaven." Acts 1:9.

A few days after the Resurrection Jesus was raised to Heaven in full sight of His disciples. Can you imagine how they must have felt?

They'd been with Him for three years or so. Saw Him preach and heal the sick. Witnessed His arrest, death and Resurrection. And now … He was gone.

They must have missed Him very badly as they walked back to their homes. Confusion, fear and doubts must have crossed their minds several times. He is gone … and He is missed.

Missing somebody is a sign that their presence had an influence on your life, your well-being and your happiness.

Their absence now has created a void in your life. An emptiness, and a longing to be with them once again.

We've all missed someone at one time or another in our lives. It is usually someone who has been kind to us.

Are we ever missed when we are no longer there? Have we done something nice to someone who will remember us and miss our presence in their lives?

NOT ONE OF US

John said to Him, "Teacher, we saw someone driving out demons in your name, and we tried to prevent him because he does not follow us."

Jesus replied, "Do not prevent him. There is no one who performs a mighty deed in my name who can at the same time speak ill of me. For whoever is not against us is for us. Anyone who gives you a cup of water to drink because you belong to Christ, amen, I say to you, will surely not lose his reward". Mark 9:38-41.

I suppose it is in our human nature to say that someone does not belong to us because he does not believe what we believe.

What Jesus is teaching us here is that if we truly believe in Him, the Son of God, then we can't possibly be against Him.

Yet, two thousand years later we still differentiate between our denomination and that of others. We say that we believe in this, and they believe in that. We know we are right, and they must be wrong because ...

Instead of rejoicing in what unites us, we waste time arguing and debating on what divides us.

Jesus also said: "In my Father's house are many rooms ..." John 14:2.

I've just realized why. It is to put each denomination in a separate room so He can have some peace and quiet without our incessant arguing.

INSOLUBLE SOLUTIONS

There are times in life when we are faced by seemingly insoluble problems. So we work hard at finding a solution. If the problem involves others we try to persuade them to our way of thinking, we disagree, we argue, and perhaps friendships are put at risk as a result.

Whilst we're struggling to find a solution, we forget that God already has the answer. And the wise thing to do is to stop for a while, pray, and hand over the problem to Him.

As we let things rest for a while, God will suggest a reasonable solution to what irks us.

I know, this will sound strange, humourous even, to an un-believer. But the realities of life are that God knows about every inconceivable problem that we can imagine; and even those outwith our imagination. And if He knows about the problems, He also knows their solutions.

He wouldn't be an omnipotent all-knowing God otherwise.

Our hesitation to hand over our problems to Him, is itself a problem of our own making – not His.

ARE YOU A SLUM?

Given a free choice, where would you rather live? In an immaculately beautiful, well-decorated, and fully appointed with every modern convenience, luxurious house in a well-sought after area of town?

Or in a decrepit, run-down, dirty, unkempt hovel, not worthy to shelter a cockroach?

Or would you prefer a house built on solid foundations and strong enough, but requiring a little care and attention and a bit of maintenance here and there?

When Jesus was raised to Heaven He sent us His Holy Spirit to dwell within us and to guide us throughout life. I mean this quite literally; not as a figure of speech.

What home does He find in us?

A pious, obedient, prayerful, loving, caring and welcoming soul?

Or a rebellious, self-assured, defiant, insolent and un-believing one?

Or are we perhaps, like most Christians, well-meaning believers, but what a realtor estate agent would describe as: "I believe, Lord; help my unbelief" (Mark 9:24) type of person?

The sort of person whose foundations are solid enough but whose structures often have to withstand the rigors of battering which life's storms and thunders throw our way. And we don't fare well in such circumstances.

Is our soul welcoming enough for our Lord to dwell within us, albeit badly in need of a lick of paint here and there, and a little attention which prayerful devotion would soon restore?

The Lord often knocks at our door. He may not find us all spick-and-span and immaculate but at least He should find us with good honest intentions. Ready to recognize our failings and willing to put them right for His sake and in thanksgiving for what He has done for us.

"Listen! I stand at the door and knock; if anyone hears my voice and opens the door, I will come into his house and eat with him, and he will eat with me." Revelation 3:20.

"How much more, then, will the Father in Heaven give the Holy Spirit to those who ask him!" Luke 11:13.

FAITH AND ACTION

What does it mean to be a Christian? To have Faith?

We proclaim we are Christians, we go to church on Sunday, other days even, we pray, and we fast perhaps. But is that enough?

When we get to meet God, will we say: "I helped in church every week. I cleaned the church and arranged the flowers. Please let me in Heaven." or "I served on the church council for years, I was responsible for the readers' rota and I read in church on Sundays many times. I typed and printed the weekly church newsletter. Please let me in."

Is this what it means to be a Christian?

Or should we be a channel of His peace as St Francis of Assisi prayed. Or help the poor and destitute as Mother Theresa did.

"My brothers and sisters, what good is it for people to say that they have faith if their actions do not prove it? Can that faith save them? Suppose there are brothers or sisters who need clothes and don't have enough to eat. What good is there in your saying to them, "God bless you! Keep warm and eat well!" — if you don't give them the necessities of life? So it is with faith: if it is alone and includes no actions, then it is dead." James 2:14-17.

WISH LIST

You must have read or heard about the wish lists of things to do before you die.

Usually they are entitled 20 things to do before you die. The number may well vary but the intention is always the same.

The list sets out such things like undertaking a parachute jump, or swimming with dolphins – always a popular one this, I can't understand why. Or seeing a blue whale, or bungee jumping, and similar adventures ranging from the normally acceptable to the outright dangerous.

I've never seen on the list of things to do before you die the wish:

To prepare to die.

What? What do you mean to prepare to die?

I mean:

"I am the way, the truth, and the life; no one goes to the Father except by me." John 14:6.

IDLE THOUGHTS

You're going along fine with life and then a thought comes into your mind. You ignore it at first hoping it will go away. But it comes back. You get on with your life, your work and with what you were doing. The thought is still there. Niggling away at your mind. Distracting you to the point of irritation.

Sometimes I wish we could shake ourselves left and right just like a wet dog does and get rid of all our troubles and our unwanted thoughts.

But we can't.

These thoughts come from nowhere and if we give them room in our minds they can slowly lead us astray from God.

We must learn to recognize them before they become hard to control. We need to be alert to their very first influences on our soul and readily turn them over to God.

For make no mistake about it; alone, we cannot overcome them.

Evil will introduce these thoughts when we least expect them or when we're at our weakest. Tired maybe, or upset about something that's just happened in our lives; whatever the occasion – as soon as we focus away from God, the devil will seize the opportunity to gain an advantage.

Turn your thoughts, whatever they are, to God always and seek His help.

The devil is a liar. John 8:44.

"Don't you see that nothing that enters a man from the outside can make him 'unclean'?" He went on: "What comes out of a man is what makes him 'unclean.' For from within, out of men's hearts, come evil thoughts, sexual immorality, theft, murder, adultery, greed, malice, deceit, lewdness, envy, slander, arrogance and folly." Mark 7:18-22.

FIRST STEPS

Have you ever watched a video of new born birds attempting to leave the nest for the first time?

The parent bird is there on nearby branches singing away: no doubt encouraging her young to take flight. They hesitate. Look around, look down at the ground which seems miles away, and then politely say to each other: "You first." "No, no, after you ..." "Ladies first, I always say."

And none of them has the courage to take off, whilst the mother is cheering heartily: "Come on, you know you can do it!"

Eventually one of the little ones gingerly jumps out of the nest, his wings flapping madly, and somehow lands safely to the ground. In time he is followed by his siblings and yet another generation takes flight and leaves the nest.

Our first steps with the Lord are no different I suppose.

We question, we analyze, we debate and then ... perhaps ... in time, we come to believe.

Eventually, we make that first step in Faith. Believing, without having all the answers. Without knowing everything about the aerodynamics of flight, or the effects of gravity as we leave the perceived safety of our nest.

God does not ask us to know everything about Him, how He thinks, how He works, and how He manages the universe. He loves each one of us individually with an everlasting Fatherly caring affection and attention that surpasses all understanding.

All He asks is that we trust Him and believe, without question and without hesitation.

His Holy Spirit will then do the rest and help us through our journey to the Father.

ONE DAY I WAS A BOY

I was reminiscing the other day when I was a boy at school and my English teacher said to me "Your grammar stinks!"

I remember being quite upset at this sudden outburst, especially since my grandma always smelled of lavender.

When I got home I told my father what the teacher had said and he asked "Which grand-mother? I know my own mother always smells of the sweetest delicate best quality Norfolk lavender. Although I'll admit your mother's mom does smell of potpourri!"

I explained that the teacher had not specified which grandma stank. So my father wrote a letter of complaint which I had to take to school with me.

My teacher replied that she had never commented on, nor would she ever presume to comment on, my family's body odour; although she suggested that I eat fewer beans!

On reading her letter my father gave me a clip round the ears. He then wrote again to the teacher apologizing for the misunderstanding and explaining that beans were less expensive than other foods.

On reading my father's letter the teacher gave me detention after school.

On the Saturday I went to Confession. Our church had an old fashioned confessional which was a wooden booth where the priest sat and the penitents would kneel on either side and confess through a small window.

I told the priest all that had happened and how it was really a non-sin on my part thus deserving a lighter penance this week. He said "Don't speak so loud I can smell your grandmother kneeling on my other side!" Although he did not specify which grandma he could smell.

Then he gave me an extra penance for speaking loudly and for drawing attention to old peoples' body odour. Which technically I had not done because it was not me who started all this; it was my English teacher who said "Your grammar stinks!"

I think the church got this whole question of confession and absolution wrong somehow. I got a penance for my teacher's sin!

Moral: So did Jesus.

WHO'S THE SOWER?

When we read the parable of Jesus about the sower and how some seeds ended on the footpath, and others on rocky ground, and others among thorns and only a few on good grounds, we think of the Word of God spread amongst many who would not listen.

But let's consider who the sower is? Is it God teaching us? Or Jesus preaching throughout the Holy Land? Or the prophets and Disciples?

The sower is of course all of these. But he is us too. Yes ... you and me.

We have a duty and responsibility to evangelize and spread the Word of God to everyone, far and wide. Not just Christians.

If the Word of God was meant for just Christians we would dig a long furrow and make sure that the seeds are planted one by one carefully in the furrow and none are wasted. But Jesus does not say that. He spread the seeds far and wide and if people do not want to listen that is their problem. Not yours.

Of course we're not all good at preaching from the pulpit, or standing in street corners, or knocking at doors telling everyone about Jesus.

But we could preach about Jesus in our actions and the way we live. Say for instance someone invites you to go fishing, or playing golf or whatever on Sunday. And you say you can't because on Sunday you're in church. That comment alone is your sermon.

If you're in a restaurant and do the sign of the Cross before eating. That alone is your sermon.

Then there's social media. How many opportunities we have there to give our own personal sermons.

We don't need to have University Degrees in theology, religion or whatever to tell others about God. There are many learned people out there with Christian blogs and websites that would put you to sleep in the first sentence. Good luck to them. They're doing a great job curing insomnia.

Our writings need only be simple and speak about our journey hand in hand with Christ as simply as we can. We never know who might visit our website and not leave a comment. To many, our blog may be the only opportunity to learn about God.

"Preach the Gospel at all times and when necessary use words." St Francis of Assisi.

INFALLIBLE POPE

So ... is the Pope infallible or not? Does he really not make any mistakes? When I was young at school and we were taught about the Pope's infallibility in Catechism class, we assumed that it meant he was good at Math and he knew all the capitals of the world. He was also good at science, languages and everything; and never made mistakes. Because he is infallible.

The Pope's infallibility is a subject sometimes raised by non-Catholics when discussing our Faith and beliefs.

What we have perhaps not made clear is what we mean by the Pope's infallibility.

In effect it means that he is totally dependable and fail-safe when pronouncing Catholic dogma which we are to accept and believe. This is known as speaking "ex cathedra" - that is, when in the exercise of his office as pastor and teacher of all Christians he defines, by virtue of his supreme Apostolic authority, a doctrine of faith or morals to be held by the whole Church.

In all of our Church's history this speaking ex cathedra has only happened twice.

In the Constitution Ineffabilis Deus of 8 December 1854, Pope Pius IX pronounced and defined that the Blessed Virgin Mary "in the first instance of her conception, by a singular privilege and grace granted by God, in view of the merits of Jesus Christ, the Saviour of the human race, was preserved exempt from all stain of original sin."

That is to say, the Virgin Mary was born without original sin.

This is not in the Bible, but a dogma of the Catholic Church.

About 100 years later, by promulgating the Bull Munificentissimus Deus, on 1 November 1950, Pope Pius XII declared infallibly that the Assumption of the Blessed Virgin Mary was a dogma of the Catholic Faith.

That is to say that she was raised to Heaven both body and soul. Her body did not decay in the ground as would happen if buried.

Again, this is not in the Bible, but Catholic dogma.

At no other time did a Pope speak ex cathedra.

WHEN ALL HOPE IS LOST

Perhaps one of the most tragic and damaging thing that can befall anyone is the loss of hope. Whatever our situation may be, if we lose hope, if we cannot see the prospect of our situation changing for the better, we are in danger of shutting down completely and accepting the inevitable outcome.

We live in difficult times. Financial crises are affecting many people. Millions are losing their jobs, their homes and their livelihood.

Those aged fifty or more would find it very difficult to find a comparable job again, if indeed they can find any job at all. More tragically, the thousands of youngsters leaving colleges and universities with good qualifications, and little prospects of employment. They feel cheated. They did what they were advised to do. They stayed in education, they worked hard, they probably amassed large debts and loans to help sustain them whilst they studied – and now there are no jobs to go to.

There are of course other circumstances which can lead us to lose hope, besides lack of work. Illness for instance, broken relationships with no prospect of reconciliation, addictions, failures etc … all can lead us to the temptation to just give up.

Where's all this leading to? – I hear you ask.

I'd like you for a moment to consider some facts.

Whatever happens in life one thing is for certain: God is still in control. He is not hiding away behind the settee crying: "Woe woe; look at what is happening out there!"

He is in total control of the situation which He has allowed to happen, and which, in most circumstances, we have created for ourselves.

The writer of the letter to the Hebrews knew what he was saying when he wrote: To have Faith is to be sure of the things we hope for (Hebrews 11).

And the important thing, whatever our circumstances, is to hold on to that Faith and to believe, in all certainty, that God is in control. And to thank Him and praise Him for being in control. To re-affirm and acknowledge our belief that He is in control.

By doing so, somehow, we open a channel for God to turn our situation to the good. I've seen this happen several times.

Think of the alternative. By turning our back on God, by ignoring Him, blaming Him even for our situation – He will hardly feel inclined to help us. Will He? Of course, He'll remain in control, waiting for us, with Fatherly patience, love and understanding, for the moment we return to Him like the prodigal son and be welcomed in His arms.

But what do you do if someone else has lost hope – even though you may not have yourself?

Preaching will not help. It may drive them further away.

Love, sympathy, compassion, whatever practical help you can offer may well help a little.

But most important is prayer. Silent prayer even. Without them knowing about it.

Let your Faith and your hope work for them. Even though they may have little or no Faith at all, your Faith is enough.

The best listened to and answered prayers are those we pray for other people. They show God our generosity of spirit, our love, our compassion, and most of all, our Faith in Him.

Don't suggest solutions to God; like: "Please help him find a job", "let him get better soon", and so on - but earnestly and in all Faith hand the situation over to Him. He knows what to do, in His time and in His own way. Just say: "Thy will be done" and mean it. And watch His miracles at work.

IT'S NOT FAIR

It's not fair. Just because I hate my greens I cannot leave the table until I've eaten all my vegetables.

It's not fair. Just because some children did something bad at school the whole class had to stay late and miss a break.

It's not fair. I can't watch TV until I've finished my homework.

It's not fair. I have to be back at home by 11 o'clock.

It's not fair. Just because other youngsters drink and drive, dad will not let me borrow the car in case I have an accident.

It's not fair. Just because some people went on strike, the company is in financial difficulties and many of us will lose our jobs.

It's not fair. They've arrested a man in the park. They've brought Him to court under false charges. They brought forward lying witnesses who made unsubstantiated claims against Him. They then beat Him up, spat on Him, placed thorns on His head, tortured Him, nailed Him to a Cross and killed Him.

It's just not fair.

PRAYERS

People sometimes ask: Why pray? Will it change the will of God, or budge Him in any way?

As parents, we do sometimes change our minds and give way to our children's demands, (eventually), especially when they go on and on about something that they want. Perhaps they make us see reason and we oblige them because we love them.

Are we to believe that our Father in Heaven loves us less than we love our own children? That He will not give us what we ask Him?

In Luke 18:2, Jesus tells the story of a widow who pestered a judge for so long that he eventually gave in and helped her. This parable teaches us not to be discouraged and always pray to God for our needs. Not what we want. But what we need.

Yet again, in the Lord's Prayer, we are taught to ask God our Father, and we will receive.

So then, how about praying to God? Will our prayers change His mind, or His will? Or are His plans for us already set out and no prayers will change them?

Over the years I have learnt that by praying, especially when praying for others, God does listen and sometimes our prayers are answered.

Whether He answers our prayers because we prayed, or He meant to answer them anyway (i.e. it was His will all along); is a debating point which can go on for ever - without us reaching a conclusion.

This is simply because we are not meant to understand Him, and to understand the reasoning behind His actions.

He is God. We are not.

We really should stop bringing Him down to our level by trying to understand Him with human minds.

However, the fact that we don't understand how, when and why our prayers are sometimes answered, and sometimes not, is not a good reason for us to stop praying.

It is sufficient to learn from Christ, who prayed to God many times, and who encouraged us to do the same.

And when we pray we should do so in thanksgiving, in hope, and in the sure knowledge that He is listening.

DOES GOD EXIST?

An atheist was spending a quiet day fishing in Scotland when suddenly his boat was attacked by the Loch Ness monster.

In a second the monster tossed him and his boat high into the air. Then it opened its mouth to swallow him.

As the man fell head over heels, he cried out, "Oh, dear God! Help me please!" At once, the ferocious attack scene froze in place, and as the atheist hung in mid-air, a booming voice from above said: "I thought you didn't believe in Me!"

"Come on God, give me a break!!" the man pleaded." Two minutes ago I didn't believe in the Loch Ness monster either!"

I wonder what it's like being an atheist. Being sure without a shadow of a doubt that God does not exist. Not only that, but also telling others that God doesn't exist; and they are wrong to believe in a "nice old man with a beard living up in the sky on a cloud!"

I believe in God. He has proved His existence to me. But try as I can I will never be able to convince someone else that God exists. This is a decision that everyone must make for themselves. They should take that first step in blind Faith and dare to believe. That's all it takes. To dare to believe that God exists and in time God will make Himself known to you.

An atheist friend of mine said that if he were to meet God he'd ask Him why He allows so much suffering in the world. I thought it amusing that this particular atheist was presuming to meet someone he does not believe in.

I answered him: "What if God asks you why YOU have allowed so much suffering around you and did nothing about it?"

It is said that hell is the complete absence of God. But if this is so, there are a number of people on this earth right now who have a complete absence of God in their lives and they seem to be doing all right.

I believe hell is being absolutely sure that God exists, without any shadow of a doubt. Knowing that God is love eternal. And then be in absolute absence of that love for eternity.

When God created man He had two choices. To create a race of robots totally submissive to His every will and doing as He commanded. Or to be given the choice to decide for ourselves.

In His immense love for His creations God gave us the choice to decide for ourselves. To return His love or not. To obey and follow His way or not.

He even gave us the freedom to believe that He does not exist, and in doing so, to shut ourselves from His love.

TELL THEM ABOUT MARY

Once upon a time there was an old priest who became rather forgetful and tired of giving sermons at Mass on Sunday.

He used to write down his sermons and then read them at Mass; but more often than not he used to forget bringing his sermons to church; so at sermon time he had nothing to read anyway.

He reasoned that if he had to write down his sermons in order to remember them, then how could the congregation be expected to remember them after leaving church.

With such impeccable logic he decided to do something about it.

One Sunday morning at Mass he announced: "I'm getting old and forgetful. I really can't be bothered anymore with writing sermons I instantly forget. So from now on there will be no more sermons at Mass!"

His congregation was very disappointed and some even complained to the Bishop.

The Bishop called the old priest in for an explanation. Somewhat pensively the old priest explained that he could no longer remember what to say in his sermons, and even though he prepared sermons in writing, he often forgot to bring his writing to church, which meant he had no sermon to deliver.

The Bishop sympathized with the elderly colleague and said: "Here's something you could try. Next time you have to give a sermon say in a loud voice 'I have an announcement to make!'

"This will ensure you have everyone's attention. They will hang on to your every word.

"Then say just as loudly 'I have fallen in love with a woman'.

"Now this will certainly have them all listening very carefully and remembering your every word.

"And then calmly tell them about the Virgin Mary, and all the good she did for us. It will be easy. Just speak from the heart of your love for Our Lady".

The old priest was overjoyed and the following Sunday he stood proudly at the lectern and said loudly:

"I HAVE AN ANNOUNCEMENT TO MAKE!"

And sure enough everyone sat up in their pews to listen very carefully. The old priest then continued just as loudly:

"THE BISHOP HAS FALLEN IN LOVE WITH A WOMAN ..."

As the congregation stirred in their seats the old priest went on:

"I can't for the life of me remember her name ..."

Many non-Catholics perhaps don't understand our devotion to Mary, the Mother of God, and often believe that our love for her is wrong and somewhat sacrilegious. They quote bits of the Bible like:

"Christ said 'I am the way, the truth, and the life; no one goes to the Father except by me.'

Or Paul's message in his letter to Timothy when he says, "there is one God, and there is one mediator who brings God and mankind together, Christ Jesus."

To pray to Mary, or any other Saint for that matter, must seem like idolatry or blasphemy to many.

But let's consider this some more.

When someone is ill, or in some difficulty, we often pray for them and ask God to come to their aid. This is right and proper and it shows our charitable loving intentions on our part; it shows our generosity of spirit and caring.

Prayers are the greatest gifts we can give to or receive from someone. God loves to hear our prayers on behalf of someone else.

When we pray for others we are mediating for them. We are putting in a good word for them with God. It's like a friend of yours giving you a good reference when you apply for a job, or an exclusive club membership.

When we pray to Mary and asking her help we are doing no different. We are asking her, or any other Saint, to put in a good word for us with God. We are not worshipping her, but asking her to mediate in the same way as we do ourselves when we pray for someone.

It is significant perhaps that Christ's first miracle, turning water into wine at the Wedding in Cana, was indeed done through the mediation of His Mother. Is this a clear signal from Christ Himself that there is nothing wrong in asking Mary to mediate or intercede for us?

When we light candles in front of Mary's statue, or place flowers, this is not idolatry. We are not worshipping the statue made of stone, or whatever material. The statue is a mere representation of what Mary might look like; it is to help us imagine who we are praying to. It is no different to us having a picture of our loved ones in our wallet or purse, or on our desk at work. We don't love the picture, but the individuals it portrays. It is a reminder of our loved ones.

Let's look at this another way.

God chose Mary to be the Mother of His only Son. He obviously had, and still has, high regard for her. She said "Yes" and bore a child whom she raised to adulthood.

Do you think that God would discard her after that as an empty insignificant shell? Or do you think He would honour her and welcome her in Heaven as a special person?

How about Jesus Himself? He is God made man. He is the personification of love, mercy and goodness. How does He regard Mary and Joseph, His earthly father? Just two people who raised Him up? Or important people worthy of a special place in Heaven?

How does Jesus regard His followers like Peter and the other disciples who set up the early church; and Paul who preached Christ's good news? Just ordinary men; or special people in Heaven?

Peter and the other disciples performed many miracles when on earth. They did not do this through their own power but in the name of Christ who honoured them and was with them through the Holy Spirit.

When they died and went to Heaven, where we all hope to go one day, did they suddenly lose their power to perform miracles and were relegated to a lower ranking of Saints?

The early Saints, and others since, still can and do perform miracles today when we ask them. Not through their own power but through God's power in honouring them.

When we pray to Mary and the Saints, we do not worship them, but ask them to mediate for us and to ask God to perform miracles where and when He sees fit to do so.

Do you think that when we get to meet God face to face He will punish us for daring to love Mary? Or Joseph? Or any of the other Saints?

It is high time that non-Catholics who accuse us of worshipping Mary and the Saints tried to understand our devotions.

And it is also high time that Catholics explained better what we mean and do when we pray to Saints and ask for intercessions.

WHAT KIND OF BUSINESS IS GOD IN?

Let's imagine a shopkeeper or a tradesman; and every time he is approached by a customer or a client he does not serve them, he ignores them and drives them away.

How long do you think this person will remain in business? Pretty soon word would spread round about his attitude and very few people, if any, would bother to go to him for his merchandise.

Let's now consider a different situation. We pray to God for help, for advice, or about some worry or trouble on our mind. We pray and pray and ... nothing. No response. Nil. Our situation, or whatever we are praying for, is still the same if not worse.

We get discouraged, we doubt, and in some cases some of us probably cease to believe altogether.

It is easy of course to sing God's praises and wave our hands in the air saying Hallelluya or whatever, when things are going well in our lives. Or type fancy slogans on our blogs or social media urging others to type Amen if they agree.

But what happens when things go wrong, really wrong. And we pray and pray and don't seem to get an answer.

Is it OK then to get a little angry and impatient with our God and tell Him honestly what's on our mind?

I think Yes. It is OK to let God know our real feelings. He can take our anger. After all, He did take our anger when hanging there on the Cross. At least we're being honest with Him and our feelings.

But let's consider this further. Getting angry with God and turning our backs on Him is hardly going to work in the long run is it? He is hardly going to be frightened into submission and give us what we pray for. All that throwing our toys out of the pram will achieve is make the devil laugh in anticipation.

Let's ask the question: What kind of business is God in?

He is hardly in the business of losing His followers; His customers or clients if we consider the scenario of the shopkeeper.

God sometimes does not respond to our prayers quickly enough or as we wished because He knows our circumstances better than we know them ourselves. And sometimes what we ask for is not right for us, or those around us, or those for whom we are praying right now.

In His own time, and in His own way, He will respond according to His will.

Our best action when things go wrong in our lives is to continue to pray and to praise Him. Yes, praise Him. Through gritted teeth even.

We are not praising God because things have gone wrong, but because He is still in control and in charge of what is happening. We acknowledge His supreme will above ours.

By praising Him we somehow help open a channel with our Creator to come to our aid.

And the harder we pray, however difficult it is, the more our Faith grows and is strengthened. Because it proves we believe there's Someone out there listening.

"Every test that you have experienced is the kind that normally comes to people. But God keeps His promise, and He will not allow you to be tested beyond your power to remain firm; at the time you are put to the test, He will give you the strength to endure it, and so provide you with a way out". 1 Corinthians 10:13.

PRAYING TO SAINTS

For years on end the discussion as to whether it is right to pray to Saints rages on. So let's see if we can clear the confusion a little.

Those who accuse Catholics of wrong doing seem to focus on two points in particular; there are others; but let's concentrate on the main two points.

It is not Biblical. Nowhere in the Bible does it say that we should pray to Saints, or that they can hear us and/or answer our prayers or intervene on our behalf.

Praying to anyone else but God is wrong. We are worshiping Saints and this is sacrilegious. Only Christ is the way to God.

Before we go on, let me make clear at this stage that Catholics do not pray TO Saints; but in fact they ask Saints to pray FOR us. The prayers are often said as a means of intercession or mediation. We ask Saints to pray to God on our behalf and to help us in certain situations.

Let's now consider the first point mentioned above – It is not Biblical.

Of course, our critics are right. Praying to Saints is not Biblical and nowhere does the Bible encourage it. The reason for this is that at the time many books of the New Testament were written the early Christians were too busy spreading God's Word and the Good News about Christ. Many died violently for their belief and their message. The word Saint had not even been invented then. It was much later that these early Christians and martyrs were considered special by the Church and worthy of special attention.

So let's look further at these people. People like Christ's earthly parents, Mary and Joseph, or His disciples like Peter, Matthew and the others, or people like Paul and Barnabas who spread the Gospel far and wide.

What happened to them when they died? Did they just turn into dust to be forgotten for ever? Or did they perhaps get welcomed to Heaven by Jesus?

At this juncture, one should point out that in all likelihood they are in Heaven, and not waiting in some Heavenly Waiting Room somewhere watching TV or reading magazines until Judgment Day.

And by the way, this bit is Biblical.

When Christ turned to the thief beside Him on the Cross He said "today you'll be in Heaven with me". He did not say "you'll have to stay in the Waiting Room a while".

So having assumed that these early "Saints", and others since, are in Heaven, we ask what are they doing there.

Is it possible that, having led a saintly life when on earth, helping others and spreading God's Word, they have now, once in Heaven, somehow become either deaf or immune to our calls for help and intercession?

When we pray to these Saints, asking them to intercede for us, do they suddenly put their hands on their ears and sing "La La Lala … La La Lala … I can't hear you because it is not Biblical to do so!"

Or is it perhaps possible that, as they have been accepted in Heaven and honoured by God for what they had done when on earth, He sometimes, in His own time, and according to His will, He grants their requests and answers our prayers in the form of a miracle perhaps; or by helping us in some way. For it is God who performs the miracles and not the Saints!

How else would you explain the many miracles at Lourdes and other Holy shrines, and those performed after prayers to many Saints?

Indeed, miracles do happen in this day and age. The trouble is few people are willing to believe in them.

And now we turn to the second point in this discussion – Praying to anyone else but God is wrong. Praying to Saints is idolatry, and so is having statues and images of them, placing flowers or lighting candles by their statues and images and so on.

I suppose a good starting point is to ask our critics whether they have a photo of their loved ones in their wallet, purse, or on their desk at work or workplace.

When they look at the photo do they actually love the piece of paper, (or image on their cell phone or tablet), or does it remind them of their loved ones and how precious they are to them?

In the same way, when Catholics pray in front of a statue or an image, they do not pray to the piece of stone or marble; but it is just a representation to remind them of what that particular Saint/individual might look like.

Placing flowers or lighting candles in no way is a sign of idolatry but just a sign of respect and reverence to the individual prayed to.

God, Christ and the Saints do not need our flowers, candles or constant prayers; in that they are in no way diminished or found wanting if we do not do these things. We do them out of respect.

Perhaps the point could be made another way. When our critics lose a loved one, do they ever visit the grave, where the name and perhaps a photo of the deceased are displayed? Do they ever place flowers on the grave? Or do they just assume that the person is dead and either in Heaven, hell or maybe in a Waiting Room somewhere?

Does placing flowers on a grave constitute idolatry? Or is it a sign of respect and love for the deceased buried there?

Do our critics keep photos in albums of their deceased loved ones? And do they remember them fondly every now and then and smile perhaps?

It is no different for Catholics. When we place flowers in front of a statue or image, when we pray to the Saints and ask for help, it is because we believe in life after death. It is because we believe these people are in Heaven. They are looking down upon us.

And they are certainly not singing "La La Lala ... I can't hear you!"

A HEAVENLY WISH

There I was face to face with St Peter. He looked at his computer monitor and said. "Yep … your credentials are OK. You've made it. Welcome to Heaven!"

I smiled silently.

He looked at me pensively and asked, "Do you know how sometimes in supermarkets they have special offers – you know, buy one and get one free?"

I nodded and said nothing, wondering what he was on about.

"Well, you're in luck," he smiled, "we have a similar offer today. Now you're accepted in Heaven you can name one other person to come in too. Whoever you name, no matter what sins they have committed, they'll all be wiped clean here on my computer, and that person can enter Heaven. Isn't that wonderful?"

I smiled again silently.

"Well, who will it be?" he asked.

I did not know what to say. Shall I get my wife up here? But then, how about my children? Which one do I choose instead? The eldest, the youngest, or the one in the middle?

How about my mom or my dad? Or one of my brothers or my sister?

Their lives are so inter-dependent. If I bring my wife here, who will look after the children left behind? And is it right and fair to bring one of the young children here before they've had a chance to live life? Will mom be able to cope without dad? Or dad without mom?

He interrupted my thoughts by saying, "You're having difficulties deciding because you see things through a human perspective. You analyze and measure things your way; often in a possessive manner.

"You say things like my wife, my children, my parents and my brothers and sister … as if these people belong to you.

"No one and nothing belongs to anybody and everything belongs to God.

"God gave life and only He decides when it ends and whether people come here or … the other place.

"When you say 'my wife', she does not belong to you. She is the woman God gave you whom you should love and honour and devote your life to.

"The children are not yours. They are a gift whom God gave you to nurture, cherish and to bring up to follow His Word.

"Your parents or sibling and family and friends are all gifts given to you by God, in the same way that you are a gift to them. We are all gifts to each other; and we should do our best to make our presence with others a cherished and memorable treasure."

I gulped and said nothing.

He smiled a little and continued.

"You humans often complain when a young life is taken or when someone leaves dependents behind with seemingly no one to care for them.

"You forget that God is there to care for them, and He leaves plenty of opportunities for those people left behind to take on the task He has set them.

"Whilst everyone has his allotted time on earth, whilst there, their main job is to do His will so that when their turn comes they end up here!

"When someone dies, it is understandable that you miss them and you grieve. The fact that you miss them means that their presence had a positive effect on your life. But you must remember that if they followed God's Word, then they'd be up here with Him for eternity.

"And that's a cause for joy, is it not?"

I nodded meekly and said nothing.

"Not everyone who calls me 'Lord, Lord' will enter the Kingdom of Heaven, but only those who do what my Father in Heaven wants them to do." Matthew 7:21.

MY EMMAUS

Just after Christ's Resurrection, two of His followers were going to Emmaus. (Luke 24: 13-35).

They were totally distraught about Jesus' death, and even though there was now news that His tomb is empty and that Christ is alive, they were still down-hearted and confused.

Jesus appeared to them on the way. They did not recognize Him. They spoke with Him and told Him their news. They said that their Lord and leader had been crucified, and there were rumours going around that He was alive again.

Jesus did not tell them who He was but explained to them the prophets' predictions about Him. He walked with them all the way to Emmaus, but still they did not recognize Him. It wasn't until He broke and blessed the bread that they recognized Him.

Why? I ask myself.

Why did they not recognize Him when they first saw Him, or when He took the time to explain to them the writings of the prophets?

Could it be that their minds were more pre-occupied with their problems and their dilemma rather than listening to Him?

You can just imagine how their mind worked and how concerned they were about their predicament.

Their leader is dead. What are they to do now? Is it all over? Every thing He said and taught comes to nothing? And what of the future? What are His followers to do now?

But aren't we just the same.

How often do events touch our lives and turn it upside down. Events perhaps of our making, or events that we did not contribute to but they affect us all the same.

And we panic. What are we to do now? What will happen next?

We fear the future, we fear matters getting out of our control and we turn our attention to our problems and our dilemma. Just like those two on the way to Emmaus.

Yet, all the time we are panicking Jesus is there. Walking beside us. Quite literally. Waiting for us to recognize Him, hold His hand in the full knowledge and trust that He will see us through our darkest hour.

It is our doubts, our fears and our worries which prevent us from seeing Him.

Copyright © 2015 by Victor S E Moubarak

Ref: 060715 – 126 – 29260 F

Printed in Poland
by Amazon Fulfillment
Poland Sp. z o.o., Wrocław